Blind
Spots

Blind Spots

The Ultimate Guide to
Building a Better Win-Loss Program

RYAN SORLEY

LIONCREST
PUBLISHING

COPYRIGHT © 2025 RYAN SORLEY
All rights reserved.

BLINDSPOTS
The Ultimate Guide to Building a Better Win-Loss Program

FIRST EDITION

ISBN   978-1-5445-4746-6 *Hardcover*
       978-1-5445-4745-9 *Paperback*
       978-1-5445-4747-3 *Ebook*

To my kiddos, Leo, Maya, and Allana: may this book inspire you to write one of your own one day! You are limitless and can do anything you put your mind to.

Contents

Introduction

"YOU'D THINK THEY'D HAVE THEIR SHIT TOGETHER GIVEN WE'RE looking to spend $40 million with them!"

This CIO was frustrated. And he had every right to be.

"Every time they come to our office for a meeting, they pull up in their fancy SUV, driver and all, and ten people pour out. It's like a corporate clown car. Am I supposed to be impressed? I'd be more impressed if any one of them could answer my basic questions. Instead, I just get blank stares. What a shit show!"

Do I have your attention? Good. Because I'm telling you my origin story here. This CIO's rant set me on an entirely new career path—and eventually led me to write this book.

When this epic venting session occurred, I was a vice president at Gartner, one of the top technology research and consulting firms in the world. Chances are you're familiar with it. This angry CIO worked for a major shoe retailer based out of Boston, not too far from where I live. He was trying to decide between two major enterprise software vendors—we'll call them Company O and Company S—and he had $40 million to spend.

The CIO thought Company O's solution was hands-down the better fit. He wanted to go with them. Hell, he was *dying* to. All he needed before signing the deal was a few answers to some reasonable questions so the shoemaker's European HQ would feel comfortable with the deal.

But he couldn't seem to get those answers. Instead, he got visit after visit from the clown car.

So, he went with Company S. He didn't like their solution as much, but they had their act together, they had a clear and concise story, and they provided straightforward answers to his straightforward questions.

As an impartial advisor at Gartner, it wasn't my job (in fact, it was forbidden) to recommend which company this CIO should select. My role was simply to provide information and expertise to help him decide for himself between one tech juggernaut and another.

But, for what it's worth, I agreed with the CIO on both fronts. Company O was clearly the better fit, but their sales team was failing miserably.

I badly wanted to tell Company O how they were messing up this deal, but as part of our nondisclosure agreement, I couldn't share any information with or provide any guidance to prospective vendors. Any feedback had to come directly from the buyer.

It was like watching a $40 million trainwreck. I saw the problem coming miles down the track, but I was powerless to stop it.

Months later, I asked the CIO how Company O had taken the news they'd lost the deal. "Who the hell knows?" he barked in his thick Boston accent, "I haven't heard a peep from those bozos since the day I told them they lost the deal. You'd think they'd want to know why!"

It was too late for Company O to salvage this deal, but I was stunned one of the world's foremost enterprise software vendors could lose out on a deal of this magnitude and never investigate what went wrong. Their own clown show led them to snatch defeat from the clutches of victory. Didn't at least one of their powers that be want to know what happened?

There had to be a way for companies like this to connect the dots, to understand what went wrong and why, to learn and grow from the experience.

That was my *Aha!* moment.

From that day forward, I vowed to dedicate my entire career to helping all the Company Os of the world learn how to be better—and how to get out of their own way. In this book, I'm going to share all the lessons I've learned along my journey.

WHAT'S A WIN-LOSS PROGRAM?

If you're reading this book, you're probably a product marketer who has been put in charge of building or growing a win-loss program within your company, even though you barely know what that means.

You probably didn't get a lot of direction on how to do this. No templates. No resources. No best practices. Oh, and no budget either. Just some vague directions on scheduling interviews and offering gift cards to respondents as bait.

There's no sugarcoating it: the odds are stacked against you. But I know product marketers like you. You're determined to soak up as much information as you can so you can get this win-loss business right.

As you set out on your hero's journey, allow me to be your humble guide. Together, we will cover a lot of ground—from program vision to program value. Along the way, I will share the pieces and parts that, when strung together, will enable you to build a program far beyond your expectations.

The journey won't be easy, but your reward will be great. Not only will you be recognized as the star you are, but the knowledge and insight you collect along the way will help arm your company to win more deals, keep clients longer, and get a leg up on the competition.

But let's back up. Why is it that you or your boss suddenly decided now is the time to launch a win-loss program? It could be a lot of reasons:

- Maybe your company is reeling after a big loss or two to an annoying competitor, and you're hungry for answers beyond what the sales organization can provide.
- Maybe your sales leaders got grilled during a leadership team meeting. When they were asked for compelling reasons for their wins and losses...well, let's just say they were light on meaningful insight, so they were forced to wing it.
- Maybe your company is in full-on fundraising mode, and the CEO needs more-concrete data to impress potential investors with their deep understanding of both the competitive landscape and your buyers.

Whatever the reason, you've been handed the job of filling this knowledge void. Somehow, some way, you now have to spin a best-in-class program that checks all the boxes.

Don't worry, you've got this.

This is your origin story, your hero moment. And it is my honor and privilege to help you navigate the road ahead.

WHY ME?

Who am I, and why have I nominated myself to be your trusty guide?

I spent over two decades in research, with the majority of that time at Gartner and Forrester Research, two leading tech-research firms. My job was to help large businesses evaluate enterprise-grade technology solutions.

In that role, I heard some stories. Oh *boy*, did I hear some stories—some even more horrifying than the Case of the Crashing Clown Car. Over and over, I heard executives at multibillion-dollar companies complain about how hard certain vendors were to work with, how their sales teams were clueless, how no one at the company seemed to know how their product actually worked. I believed these executives, but I also knew that these vendors, for the most part, were great companies with excellent solutions. They were losing deals due to problems they could easily solve—that is, if they knew those problems existed.

After my *Aha!* moment, I decided to step away from the world of technology research and niche down into the field of win-loss analysis. It was criminal that organizations like Company O had such massive blindspots in their intelligence infrastructure, and I was determined to eliminate them by helping these companies build mature win-loss programs.

To bring my vision to life, in 2014, I launched DoubleCheck Research. For eight years, DoubleCheck helped well over a hundred business-to-business (B2B) technology and services clients build win-loss programs capable of delivering real, actionable insights into their organizations. In 2022, I sold DoubleCheck to Klue, the leading competitive-enablement platform provider and a company I'd long admired and partnered with. Today, I am a Klue co-founder and vice president of our win-loss division.

At Klue, we combine the power of competitive enablement with that of win-loss analysis. It's like merging superpowers (cue nostalgic "Wonder Twin powers" reference). Every day, I'm grateful to collaborate with brilliant, passionate colleagues who share my enthusiasm for helping B2B teams overcome blindspots, make data-driven decisions, and drive real, measurable change. The passion in our team is downright contagious!

THE JOURNEY BEGINS

In the following chapters, I'll walk you step by step through the process of establishing a win-loss program in your organization—from securing buy-in to navigating common challenges and pitfalls to designing and conducting professional interviews to making use of all your wonderful win-loss data once you've collected it.

Right now, building a win-loss program may seem like just one more to-do on a long list. By the end of this book, you'll understand that an effective win-loss program is so much more than that, a vessel not only for creating real value within your organization but also raising your own profile along the way.

If it sounds like a lot, it is. But if you're ready to embrace your new role and set out on your hero's journey, come meet me in Chapter 1.

PART 1

Getting Started

CHAPTER 1

What Is Win-Loss Analysis?

TELL ME IF THIS SOUNDS FAMILIAR.

You're a few weeks out from the quarterly leadership team meeting. Your boss asks you to put together a presentation on the company's current win and loss trends and be prepared to present the data, along with some recommendations. To support your effort, your boss is kind enough to shoot you an email containing a win-loss report they generated from your customer relationship management (CRM) system's reason-code data.

As you open the file, you feel a pit open in your stomach and cold sweat form on your brow.

The data is...well, garbage. It's incomplete, inconsistent, and inaccurate.

This puts you in somewhat of a bind. After all, there's no way in hell you're going to be able to take this dumpster fire and transform it into something compelling and actionable for your leadership team. If you do present any findings based on this dataset, you know failure is certain.

There will be no disasters on your watch, you decide. Better to bite the bullet and be up-front about the state of your data.

On the day of the meeting, you walk in, swallow hard, and state that you will be unable to share any reliable insights. The problem? The process of collecting, organizing, and analyzing your win-loss data is critically flawed. What little information you have is basically useless, and if your organization were to act on any of the "trends" your analysis uncovered, it may cause more damage than progress.

Your leadership team agrees. In fact, they're grateful you spoke up. They had no idea there was such a fundamental gap in their intelligence. But now that they do, they want *you* to fix it.

Yep, that's right—you've just been given the chance to build out and lead your very own win-loss program.

It's a great opportunity. And you know better than anyone how badly your company needs it. There's just one problem: you've never built a win-loss program before. You've never even been involved in one. In fact, if you're being honest, you're not fully sure what a win-loss program *is*, let alone what one looks like or how you can leverage it to help your business.

Here's your chance to learn. This chapter will break down the basics of what a win-loss program is, the problem with how most companies go about creating one, and what a good win-loss program can ultimately accomplish.

THE BASICS

At its most basic level, a win-loss program is a method for understanding why you're winning and losing deals so you can identify opportunities to improve your overall win rate—the total percentage of deals you close. Through a series of interviews and surveys with related buyers, your win-loss team works to uncover what happened within a set of deals to better understand emerging trends, challenges, and opportunities.

A win-loss program isn't just learning what happened in one deal with one buyer. It's building a detailed understanding of your organization's strengths and weaknesses across a number of deals.

Each interview produces a set of qualitative, unstructured data. That interview data is then structured, analyzed, and summarized until a clear narrative emerges. Those findings are then compared to the findings from other similar interviews to identify themes, insights, and opportunities.

For instance, through just a single set of interviews, you may discover several companies that recently evaluated your offerings were all looking to leave the same main competitor. An insight like that could add tremendous value to your business. Working off this information, leadership could direct the sales team to call into each account where that competitor is the incumbent and create FUD (fear, uncertainty, and doubt) by raising the pain points mentioned during your interviews. Beyond this example, similar information regularly helps organizations identify and leap at new opportunities, invest in key strategic areas of business, and ultimately improve their win rates.

These revelations aren't limited to sales-enablement activities either. A robust win-loss program can add value across your organization and benefit strategic planning, product-roadmap development, go-to-market (GTM) messaging and reputation management, pricing strategies, competitive intelligence, and other areas.

YOU ALREADY HAVE A WIN-LOSS PROGRAM

Now that you know the basics of what a win-loss program is, I have some good news and some not-so-good news.

First, the good news: whether you or your organization realizes it or not, you already have a win-loss program. Yay!

Now, the bad news, and I know you already know this: your win-loss program probably isn't very good. At best, it's a collection of half-completed fields and dropdowns your sales team hastily enters into the CRM system.

Sure, it's tempting to shrug your shoulders and say that some data is better than no data, and in some cases, you could even be right. But here's the thing: when the bulk of your win-loss data comes from sales, as it does in most programs, you have no way of guaranteeing that data is accurate.

In fact, in our experience, it probably isn't. To understand why, let's take a closer look at the key challenges of a typical sales-sourced win-loss research program.

CHALLENGE #1: THE WRONG PERSON FOR THE JOB

Most salespeople work for commission. The more time they spend filling out win-loss fields in their CRM system, the less time they spend selling. Especially if they're working for a fast-paced, high-pressure sales organization, it's unlikely they'll want to take the time to complete yet another administrative task, let alone make sure they complete it accurately.

With this in mind, many organizations build a set of simple reason codes the salesperson can select from a dropdown menu in their CRM system (which I'll talk about more in the next section). This lessens the burden on the salesperson, but it's still an administrative task they would rather do without. The result? Many salespeople select a reason code they know may not be quite right just to complete their administrative responsibility and move on.

This begs the question: couldn't you solve the problem by incentivizing your salespeople to take their time and be more thoughtful?

Nice try, but no. More thoughtful answers *might* get you closer to more accurate data, but it won't get you all the way. Why? Because salespeople often don't know why they won or lost a deal, or they aren't self-critical enough to ask themselves some hard questions. It's much easier to say you lost a deal based on price than it is to say, "I lost the deal due to my inability to sell," or, "I was super aggressive. I completely turned off the buyer, and they'll never do business with us again, ever."

I don't say this to fault salespeople. After all, I am a salesperson and have been for over twenty-five years. My point is this kind of critical self-reflection and vulnerability are, well, challenging for all of us.

Ultimately, that's the big problem here. It's fundamentally unfair to rely on your sales team to conduct their own win-loss interviews and self-report the results. And in terms of challenges, that's just the tip of the iceberg.

CHALLENGE #2: AN UNRELIABLE TOOL

Reason-code dropdown menus might seem like good, useful time-savers, but often, they're anything but. In fact, most options in a reason-code dropdown are rigid, dated, and incomplete, failing to provide sales with a solid list of options that align with the many real-world scenarios they encounter.

Nothing good can come from equipping a busywork-averse sales team with an outdated set of reason codes. First, the data is simply too high-level. Any analyst or executive team hoping to learn more about why they keep losing deals on price would end up with more questions than answers. Reason-code systems are not set up to capture the detailed story of what went right or wrong with a deal. They are only able to create a handful of graphs and charts based on those reason-code selections.

Second, and perhaps most importantly, the data is unreliable. As already discussed, the person inputting the data (the salesperson) is an unreliable source of information, and the reason codes themselves are inherently limited. It's not just that you're getting an incomplete picture—you could be getting a wholly inaccurate and misleading picture. (Danger, Will Robinson!)

I would caution any leadership team against using sales-sourced reason-code data to make important decisions. And yet, unfortunately, big decisions based on bad data are made every day, often leading organizations down the wrong path. The worst part? No one realizes their mistake—at least, not until it's far too late to do anything about it.

CHALLENGE #3: MISINFORMATION

Regardless of how the deal turns out, sellers often skip conducting even basic win-or-loss interviews. Sometimes, they'll circle back and speak with the buyer to learn what happened, but most often, they just move on to their next deal. Typically, if they win, they do a little dance and leave it at that. If they lose, they chalk it up to whichever reason code most closely resembles their personal view of why they lost. If none of the reason codes come close, they simply select the most popular choice: "Other."

Believe it or not, this might be a good thing. Even if the seller *did* get their buyer on the phone, that conversation may not be especially valuable. Why? Because buyers often curb their feedback and only provide the seller with a partial view of their reasons for working or not working with the seller's company.

To understand why, let's consider the dynamics.

For many of us, when we're in a relationship that's on the outs, our primary goal is to move on in a quick and amicable way. To do that, typically we withhold the full truth. We say only what we need to say and then move on. You can call this the "It's not you, it's me" syndrome.

The buyer/seller dynamic is no different. Put yourself in the buyer's shoes for a moment. In your eyes, the deal died the second that salesperson went around you and called your boss in an effort to improve their chances of closing that deal. That call crossed a line, and you're still pissed about it.

But are you going to tell the salesperson that? Is it worth stoking those flames and suffering through an awkward conversation? Probably not. Instead, you give them a vague answer. "The price was too high." "The product was missing a key feature." Anything to get this salesperson off the phone so you can get on with your life.

Inevitably, whatever partial truth you utter becomes the salesperson's reality. Satisfied with your answer, they select the appropriate option in the dropdown menu and close the book on the deal. It's no surprise, then, that when it comes to win-loss reporting, most of the time, your salesperson is just unknowingly misinformed.

To gauge the reliability of your sales-generated CRM data, consider sending a short, anonymous survey to your sales team asking the following two questions:

1. When selecting a closed won/lost reason code in our CRM system, how often do you:
   a. Find what you're looking for?
   b. Pick something because there is no choice that aligns with your situation?
   c. Pick something randomly because you have no idea why you won or lost?

2. What reason codes do you believe are missing from the current list of options?

Pay careful attention to these answers. If your sales team responds that they're usually able to find the right reason code and nothing much is missing, congratulations! Your CRM data is in good shape! Or your sales team didn't want to admit they may be fudging their selections.

In honest responses, you should see a mix of a, b, and c. And you should definitely see at least a few suggestions for Question 2. If you don't have either of these things, you may want to have a more extensive chat with your sales team.

YOU DON'T KNOW WHAT YOU DON'T KNOW

Now that we've explored the key challenges inherent in a typical ad hoc, sales-sourced win-loss program, let's put all the pieces together:

- The sales team is generally motivated by selling, not by completing administrative tasks such as win-loss reporting.
- Most reason-code efforts are inherently flawed, with the reason codes themselves being rigid, limited, and outdated.
- Buyers often don't share the real reasons and motivations behind their decisions with the salesperson directly.

- Disparate, anecdotal data may provide some insight into how individual deals were won or lost, but they reveal very little in terms of long-term trends or themes.

Add those factors together, and it's pretty easy to see the challenges associated with a typical win-loss program that relies on the sales team for its data and intelligence. If you can't rely on a basic set of facts, how can you possibly be expected to provide any meaningful, actionable insights into why you're winning or losing business?

Short answer: you can't. At best—and this is being super optimistic—the flawed data produced by a typical in-house win-loss program allows you to study the very tip of the iceberg. Meanwhile, all the most valuable information is lurking beneath the surface.

To show you what I mean, let's look at a couple of examples of the kinds of insights a well-developed win-loss program generates.

THE NO-DECISION

When an organization is not selected, often it has no idea who it lost out to. The organization assumes a competitor outbid it, but rarely does anyone circle back to find out who the buyer ultimately chose.

Here's a little secret: quite often, the buyer didn't choose anybody. The deal ended in a no-decision.

No-decisions tend to be overlooked by many win-loss program owners, who are more focused on deals that resulted in a competitive win or loss. And yet, between 40 and 60 percent of all deals end in no-decisions.[1] This means your competitors aren't your biggest obstacle to closing a deal. You are. Often, no-decisions happen because your team didn't demonstrate time-based, measurable value significant enough to compel the buyer into action.

A properly structured win-loss interview can help your organi-

---

1   Matthew Dixon and Ted McKenna, "Stop Losing Sales to Customer Indecision," *Harvard Business Review*, June 24, 2022, https://hbr.org/2022/06/stop-losing-sales-to-customer-indecision.

zation uncover a variety of key themes and opportunities. Many of these opportunities are low-hanging fruit, where quick adjustments can drive positive change in your organization.

No-decisions are a great example of this low-hanging fruit. When you know why things stalled out and that your buyer is still in the market, you have an opportunity to get that deal back on track. After conducting thousands of win-loss interviews, our team has seen some version of the following conversation countless times:

Interviewer: We understand you decided not to move forward with us. Did you choose to go with another provider?

Buyer: No. We never made a decision.

Interviewer: Why is that?

Buyer: Well, it wasn't the right time. We liked the seller, but it didn't look like they had [Feature X] yet, and that was a deal killer for us.

This kind of insight is a game-changer. Maybe you *do* have Feature X and just failed to highlight it during your presentation, or maybe you've come out with Feature X since you last connected with the buyer. In either case, you now have the opportunity to reach back out to the buyer and reignite the conversation.

But the insights don't stop there. If you learn other buyers also chose not to work with you for the same reason, you've likely identified an important trend. With this insight, you now know what to prioritize with the next iteration of your product—which I define in this book as any service, platform, offering, solution, etc. you might be selling.

Scenarios like this are a big reason win-loss programs have so much value. After all, getting just one or two no-decisions back on track may mean hundreds, thousands, or even millions of dollars in additional revenue for your company.

And it doesn't stop with no-decisions. Win-loss interviews reveal all kinds of surprises that lead organizations to make important micro and macro adjustments. Let's look at a quick example from my own history.

THE WILDCARD FACTOR

My company conducted a win interview for a client who had recently beaten out a competitor for a big contract. In the client's eyes, the win was a perfectly executed slam dunk. As we dug deeper, however, we learned the deal could just as easily have gone the other way. Far from being a slam dunk, it was a real nail-biter.

The client's win didn't come as a result of a superior sales experience or stellar product. Sure, they did have experience and a decently dialed-in product, but so did their competitors. Instead, the detail that tipped the deal in their favor came from the unlikeliest of places: a bedtime conversation between spouses.

One night, the buyer was lying in bed with her husband, a partner at a venture capital firm. Her laptop was open, and they got to talking about work. That's when she told him her problem: essentially, her company was down to two different marketplace vendors to help support their global expansion efforts, and she couldn't pick between the two.

The husband looked at the two candidates, then pointed to our client. "We recently reviewed a pitch deck from this company," he said. "We didn't invest in them, but we were impressed by their leadership team and vision. I think they might be a really good fit for you."

And that's how our client won the deal—just a little nudge in the right direction from a chance conversation between spouses.

When we shared this insight with our client, their jaws dropped. That wasn't the answer they expected. Not. At. All.

Their ability to build strong relationships won them that deal, but their overconfidence almost sunk it. Now that their win-loss program had revealed the truth, they had the opportunity to shake off the curse of overconfidence and approach every deal with a heightened level of rigor and attention to detail.

THE BENEFITS ARE YOURS FOR THE TAKING

When all is said and done, the purpose of a win-loss program is to improve your organization's win rate, which in turn contributes to revenue growth and market-share improvement.

To reach that goal, your win-loss program must benefit not only the sales team, but every other functional group within the organization as well. Sure, all roads ultimately lead back to sales, but to close those deals, organizations must equip their salespeople with all the tools and information they need to be successful.

This means providing your sales team with current information about all your products and services. It means providing robust competitive intelligence so they know exactly how your offerings differ from your competitors'. It means being able to clearly articulate packaging and pricing as it aligns with each buyer's use case. It means understanding the buying motion of the organization and adapting to it so the sales process feels like a partnership and not a transaction.

That's a lot to learn—way more than a set of outdated reason codes could ever reveal.

To build a win-loss program that actually works—and provides your leadership team with the trends, insights, and opportunities they've been craving—it's time to shift from the default sales-sourced model and start bringing the whole organization into the conversation. In the next chapter, I'll show you the different forms your win-loss program could take.

ACTIONS & TAKEAWAYS

1. Take stock of your current win-loss program efforts.

2. Determine and document current data inputs. Where is your current win-loss data coming from?

3. Review your reason codes. How confident are you in them and the data they produce?

4. Determine your internal audience. Who are you doing this work for?

5. Determine which research areas are most important to you. What research areas might other internal stakeholders be interested in?

CHAPTER 2

Stages of Maturity

COMPANY X WAS EAGER TO PUT A WIN-LOSS PROGRAM IN PLACE. When I asked why they chose now to start building out their win-loss program, the program's champion said, "Competition. Company Y and Company Z are hot on our heels, and we need a leg up."

"Interesting," I replied. "I've never heard of Company Y or Company Z, but that's good to know."

The very next week, guess who reached out to us about our win-loss services?

That's right, Company Y, who *also* wanted to launch a win-loss program.

This kind of situation happens *all the time*. First, one company calls us, then their competitor calls us, then another competitor calls us, and so on. (In this case, Company Z never did reach out to us, but you never know.)

In many industries, such as tech, manufacturing, and financial services, a good win-loss program has become table stakes. Adopt a win-loss program, and you'll stay relevant and competitive. Pass on building a win-loss program—or do nothing—and you risk losing time, money, and market share.

If you're responsible for win-loss within your organization and you've personally decided to do nothing, you may be single-handedly holding your company back from winning more deals. Worse, you probably don't even know it.

By building out a win-loss program for your company, you're either catching up or pulling ahead. A well-run win-loss program not only helps your company improve its win and renewal rates and beat expectations, it also has the potential to provide cross-organizational benefits—increased revenue, reduced sales-cycle time, and improved market share.

But you have to do it. And you have to do it *right*. Otherwise, what's the freaking point?

In this chapter, you'll learn how to assess your win-loss program's current state using the maturity model we developed at DoubleCheck during my early work in win-loss analysis.

By evaluating where your company's win-loss program currently is, understanding where you want to go, and getting a better sense of where your competitors might be, you'll be able to remove a few common blindspots and start driving action.

Typically, I've found a company's win-loss program falls into one of four levels (see Figure 1.1):

- **Sales-Sourced.** No formal win-loss program. The sales team collects a partial view into the buyer's experience with no formalized plan for acting on the insights gathered.
- **Siloed.** Single-department win-loss effort focused on collecting information from buyers for a specific area of the business. Often, there is no formal plan for taking action.
- **Integrated.** Holistic program effort where an organizational program owner is assigned to collect data from buyers in all areas related to their evaluation experience.
- **Action-Oriented.** Strategic stakeholder group is assigned to review the cross-functional buyer insight collected and build and execute a priority action plan to drive measurable, positive change.

While each program profile has a place, there are pros and cons to each. Let's take a closer look.

Four stages to win-loss program maturity

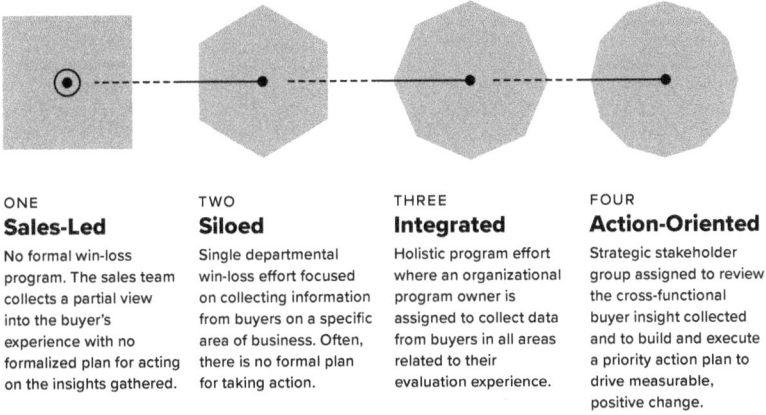

ONE	TWO	THREE	FOUR
Sales-Led	**Siloed**	**Integrated**	**Action-Oriented**
No formal win-loss program. The sales team collects a partial view into the buyer's experience with no formalized plan for acting on the insights gathered.	Single departmental win-loss effort focused on collecting information from buyers on a specific area of business. Often, there is no formal plan for taking action.	Holistic program effort where an organizational program owner is assigned to collect data from buyers in all areas related to their evaluation experience.	Strategic stakeholder group assigned to review the cross-functional buyer insight collected and to build and execute a priority action plan to drive measurable, positive change.

Figure 2.1

STAGE ONE

Sales-Led

Win-Loss Program

People	Process	Data Capture & Distribution	Benefits
Informal post-decision call with buyer for personal knowledge gain. Most often conducted by sales lead or the sales manager.	No standard interview questions or approach, and little to no formal sharing of findings.	Data may or may not be captured in CRM or shared via email. Calls are not recorded or transcribed.	Stage 1 insight helps an individual salesperson or team identify areas of opportunity for improvement, and to get a sense of what may have gone right or wrong during the sales process so that they can adjust their approach during future opportunities.

Figure 2.2

In the sales-sourced approach, there is no formal win-loss program in place. This is what most organizations have. The sales team collects a partial view into buyers' experiences with no formalized plan for acting on the insights gathered. In many cases, the data is sourced from the salespersons' selection in a reason-code dropdown menu within their CRM system (see Chapter 1).

This is also the most common level companies are at when they reach out to me. Typically, on our first call, the product marketer will say something along these lines: "We don't know why we're winning and losing. We're asking sales, but I don't trust a word they say. We need to hear from our buyers, and we need an unbiased and independent study to help us get to the heart of what's happening."

To be clear, these sales teams aren't bad or inherently untrustworthy. As I talked about in Chapter 1, the problem with a sales-sourced win-loss program is you're asking your sales team to do work outside their wheelhouse. They don't have all the tools, training, or information required to determine why they won or lost a sale, let alone have meaningful discussions with their buyers about the outcome.

But that's not the only problem. Beyond sales, businesses following a sales-sourced model often lack a formal process or structure to collect and organize the information they do gather. So, not only does sales provide incomplete and often biased data, no one's doing anything meaningful with said data anyway. Even worse, everyone *knows* the data is unreliable, but no one has the time or inclination to fix it. Not ideal.

The best thing you can say about Level 1 is at least it's better than nothing. But that's pretty faint praise.

To level up your Level 1 program:

1. **Make it about the buyer.** This is the real learning opportunity. Even in an informal interview, ask your buyer to share open and honest feedback about why your company was or was not selected.

2. **Hold sales accountable.** The sales team must understand their job does not end when they close a deal; they still need to collect feedback from buyers and input that feedback somewhere it can be accessed.

3. **Enable easy sharing.** If you're sticking with a sales-sourced program, the product marketing team should enable the sales team by designating a central location where they can document their findings, such as Slack, Google Drive, Klue, or your CRM system. Further, sales leadership needs to hold the sales team accountable for executing on that request and having that discussion.

Improving in this area takes discipline and proactivity. The sales team must regularly have conversations with buyers about why your company was or was not selected. Then, they must document that feedback in a way that's useful to any further postmortem deal review. If you can do that, you may even have an opportunity to perform some cursory trends analysis. Sure, the data is likely to be narrowly focused on product feedback, pricing feedback, and maybe some sales experience, but at least you have some reliable information to work with.

Once you've leveled up your sales-sourced win-loss program, you'll have overcome some of the inherent shortcomings of this approach. From there, you'll have an entirely new set of challenges to consider.

THE VERDICT

A sales-sourced win-loss interview is better than nothing—although the salesperson's bias, focus on objection handling, and true interest in getting the deal back on track will often lead to awkward moments in the conversation and create anything but a safe environment for that buyer to share meaningful and constructive feedback. Instead, the buyer often limits their feedback to avoid debate while seeking the closest exit.

STAGE TWO

Siloed

Win-Loss Program

People	Process	Data Capture & Distribution	Benefits
Departmental point-of-contact leads narrow, department-specific interviews directly with buyers.	Core department-specific interview questions created and findings shared primarily within that department.	Basic interview notes captured and made available within a shared document, with findings discussed primarily within that department.	If you're looking for solid insight into your specific functional area, such as product management, then the Siloed approach may fit the bill. The challenge is that your view will be limited to your piece of the puzzle, which may not provide a truly balanced view of why you won or lost the deal.

Figure 2.3

In a siloed win-loss program, certain teams within an organization have taken specific steps to answer specific questions and satisfy their specific needs. To do that, they've created a more formal win-loss program, which is a good thing, but it's narrowly focused on answering these teams' key questions. The primary beneficiaries are members of the team that designed the program, not the rest of their organization. No one else gets anything they might want—even if there are natural opportunities to do so.

Say that Sara, the head of product management, wants to build a better understanding of how buyers think about their user interface (UI)—especially as it compares to other products on the market. To get that data, Sara runs a targeted win-loss study, asking buyers why they did or did not buy from her company, what they thought about the product's UI, and how it aligned with their needs or vision.

Good for Sara. She took the initiative to learn some valuable information about the company's product. But there were a ton of other questions she could have asked while she had the buyer on the phone:

- How was the sales experience?
- What other competitors did you consider, and what were their strengths and weaknesses?
- What have you heard about us?
- Why were you looking for this solution in the first place?

By asking a few more questions, the head of product management could have gained valuable data for sales, marketing, and competitive intelligence. Instead, she only collected data that served her department's narrow self-interests. To be fair, this probably wasn't intentional. Like leaders of many teams, the head of product management probably just forgot to consider how her research could help others.

Okay, that's not too bad, right? No, but consider the optics. Imagine Sara is in an evening leadership team meeting. Everyone is tired, and you can hear more than a couple stomachs growling. Suddenly, there's a knock on the door. A delivery person hands Sara a bag containing a couple food containers.

They smell delicious.

Sara thanks the delivery person, walks back to her seat at the table, and proceeds to unpack the contents of the containers. Then, without saying anything or offering anything to anyone, she digs in.

A few minutes later, Sara is full. It's clear she ordered more food than she could stomach, and there's a lot left over. Instead of offering the leftovers to any of the other tired and hungry people in the room, she packs it all up and throws it in the trash.

Sara is full and satisfied, but everyone else is even hungrier than before. In fact, they're verging on hangry. And besides, now the room smells like garlic, olive oil, and well-seasoned chicken.

So, what's the takeaway? By not sharing, Sara may have inadvertently harmed her leadership team's ability to learn, grow, and trust each other as a unit. Everyone could have benefitted with just a little extra consideration. Instead, only one person did—and not even to the full extent she could have.

That's ultimately what you're doing when you're running a siloed win-loss program. It may feel innocent enough, but in reality, it's a big missed opportunity for other groups within the organization. That said, a siloed effort is more structured than a sales-sourced program is likely to be. At this level, we start to see some formality in the process, including a demonstration of forethought and preplanned objectives.

In a Level 2 win-loss program, your product team is deliberately calling the buyer and learning from them. You've likely thought through some questions to ask, but the effort is still a bit unstructured. Similarly, you have rudimentary tools for capturing and analyzing intelligence, such as old-school pen and paper or a customer-centric spreadsheet. You may even have a set of learning objectives and a specific use case for the research findings. While siloed programs are not perfect, you can bet the group that initiated the research effort knows a heck of a lot more now about their area than they did at the start of the effort.

Product teams are the most common repeat offenders here. They naturally want to know what people think about their solution, and they're not just asking people who are in recent win-loss situations; they're asking clients as well. In fact, their body of research might even expand outside the boundaries covered by a traditional win-loss program.

And yet, despite all the valuable data they've collected, they don't always make the effort to share what they've learned. That's too bad. As we'll see in Level 3, if your organization can get better at sharing knowledge, that's where the real magic happens.

THE VERDICT

Siloed programs can be ongoing, but typically, they're project-based with defined start and end dates. For example, you may collect intelligence, conduct an analysis, and present your findings for a mid-year meeting. Such a program will inform your strategy and determine where to invest in the upcoming year. While there's always a place for project-based research, ongoing research is a critical success factor for the win-loss space. Buyer preferences and the competitive landscape change so often in many industries that to take a snapshot of a moment in time is not enough to keep a pulse on the shifting in the marketplace. This narrow view only benefits short-term decision-making. It's like picking up a newspaper from December 1, 1980, to learn anything useful or applicable about the present day.

STAGE THREE

Integrated
Win-Loss Program

People	Process	Data Capture & Distribution	Benefits
Building upon the Integrated stage program, senior leaders sponsor a stakeholder task force created to review findings, prioritize, and drive action in the Action-Oriented stage.	Cross-functional interview guide and online survey written, with findings shared across function groups, including sales, product, and marketing.	Interviews are recorded and transcribed, online survey responses are collected, and data is stored and managed centrally.	Companies in Stage 3 may gain a holistic view of organizational opportunities and challenges across product, marketing, sales, sales engineering, and competitive and market intelligence. Oftentimes, Integrated organizations find the research to be interesting, but may not have a plan or mechanism in place to leverage the findings to take action.

Figure 2.4

With an integrated win-loss program, program owners have figured out there is an opportunity to centralize research efforts and serve the needs of all groups. If Level 1 and Level 2 leave a lot of value on the table, Level 3 is where your organization can start to turn the corner and find more benefit.

At Level 3, the decision has been made to view win-loss at an organizational level—rather than a siloed level—to serve many masters with the win-loss program and corresponding data it generates. Whether someone steps up or is assigned to the role, the program owner is responsible for reaching out to the people who used to live in silos to say, "Hey product team/sales/marketing/competitive intelligence/customer service, what are you looking to learn through an ongoing win-loss program effort?"

At this level, your organization builds a program to serve all of its needs, starting by listening and building a set of agreed-upon goals and learning objectives for the program. Based on these collective objectives, you can start conducting research, building tools to collect data, and gathering intelligence to perform trend analysis more broadly.

An integrated win-loss program also likely has executive-level buy in. The C-suite or senior leaders within the organization have an interest in the outcome, so they've given it their blessing. They may not read every interview summary, but they'll be there when you present findings on a quarterly basis because they find it interesting and well-aligned to their objectives. They may also be thinking about how to turn that data into some sort of action.

At this point, there's also some process, structure, and method in place for conducting interviews and capturing the resultant data. Within an integrated win-loss program, you begin to record and transcribe interviews, generate more consistent interview-summary reports, and create research deliverables that people can depend on. The information is distributed more broadly; instead of sharing data with just one team, the program managers make sure this information gets into the hands of anyone who might need it to make important decisions.

Those decisions drive positive change that leads to positive outcomes, such as recognizing salespeople who do well or learning from losses. Or, for example, if a buyer says a salesperson wasn't very responsive and didn't appear to show true interest in their business, their manager can say, "Let's set up some sort of plan so you can show me how you're going to be more passionate about what you're selling, so we can draw in more people to sign up with us."

As you can see, Level 3 has a lot going for it. But here's the key difference between a Level 3 program and a Level 4: in a Level 3 program, you have a strong system in place to collect data and learn from it. You may even be acting on what you're learning, but that action is more informal or organic. You're not yet taking full advantage of all the tremendous insights and opportunities you're discovering.

Other pieces may be missing as well. Leaders may not be all-in on the program, and they may not know what to do with the data. They may know they need a win-loss program, but they treat it as another checklist item; they don't have a clear vision of the endgame. As a result, their attitude becomes, "We'll worry about it when we get there." Then, when they get there, they're busy and don't know what to do with the data because they haven't discussed how to unpack its value.

To take your Level 3 program to a Level 4, the people with the most influence in your organization must have a sense of ownership and excitement about the program. If they're not eager to take the ball and run with it rather than just going through the motions, the program will never quite live up to its full potential.

This is a big deal because the stakes are a lot higher here. Levels 1 and 2 may have a lot of problems, but they also involve less effort, so the stakes are lower. Program managers invest a lot more time and resources into a Level 3 program—having meetings, coordinating across departments, asking questions, collecting data, and so on. It would be a shame to see all that time, energy, and data wasted because leadership isn't fully bought in.

Ultimately, it's that buy-in that drives the kind of action that affects outcomes. I see this firsthand with the clients I work with. One of my clients, for instance, was thrilled with the win-loss program I helped them develop. The program manager—in this case the head of competitive intelligence—would regularly meet with her leadership team to present the data I'd collected and analyzed for her. The leadership team was ecstatic, both with the findings and her work. Naturally, she was thrilled to be noticed and appreciated for the effort, but at the same time, she was also frustrated. Despite the considerable insights and opportunities she brought to the table, the program led to very little direct action.

Compare that to another client, the director of product marketing at another B2B software company, who ran an integrated program. This director had a specific goal to collect siloed intelligence on how people were responding to his company's pricing model as compared to their competitors' models. He knew he could use that slice of data to his advantage, taking it back to the leadership team and saying, "We need an investment in pricing. We need to rethink our market pricing strategy. Here's the data to support that." Ultimately, he got the approval and budget to hire a full-time pricing manager as part of his team, and that person became responsible for looking at pricing strategy and thinking through how the company should position its offerings. This investment in a new pricing person helped turn things around for the company and even improved its ability to communicate with potential buyers around price.

In this case, the director was still running a siloed win-loss program, but he was able to use that program to drive results. That's a specific action and outcome within an integrated program that directly benefited the business. Now, imagine what would happen if leadership were bought into these programs. That's where the *real* change happens.

THE VERDICT

If you're at Level 3 as an organization, it's not perfect, but you're likely fairly happy overall. You could even be driving change! That said, buckle up. The real action starts in Level 4.

LEVEL 4: ACTION-ORIENTED

STAGE FOUR

Action-Oriented

Win-Loss Program

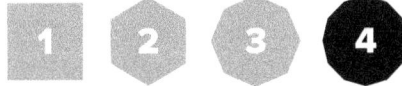

| 1 | 2 | 3 | **4** |

People	Process	Data Capture & Distribution	Benefits
Building upon the Integrated stage program, senior leaders sponsor a stakeholder task force created to review findings, prioritize, and drive action in the Action-Oriented stage.	Cross-functional interview guide is leveraged, stakeholder committee meets quarterly to review new data, determine/take action, track progress against actions, and measure results.	Centralized data is analyzed to identify trends across periods, buyer groups, products, sales regions, and competitors. The data is used to benchmark the performance of various internal groups and external companies.	Stage 4 is the holy grail of Win-Loss programs, turning insight into action that drives positive change and results in win-rate improvements. To become Action-Oriented, your leadership team must consider Win-Loss to be of strategic importance and integrate quarterly reviews of the data into their management cadence.

Figure 2.5

No matter what level you're operating at with your win-loss program, you're going to get some value out of the effort. That said, if you can get there, Level 4 is where you want to be. Here, program managers have truly operationalized their win-loss program and built an action-plan framework to manage it. In other words, not only is the data collected, your organization takes very specific, measurable actions as a result of that data.

Again, the two big differences between a Level 3 and a Level 4 program are leadership and action. Level 3 programs are still likely a bottom-up effort—even if leadership ultimately buys in. At Level 4, leadership will often initiate the program themselves. They fully back the effort, they have a vested interest in the findings, and they're ready to drive action based on the results. Because of that, they're ready to do things right.

A Level 4 program can also be driven by a board of advisors (investors), with the program's leadership presenting data up the chain as well as down. I often see this with private equity clients who put a program in place within one of their portfolio companies.

Whatever the case, the result is an actively engaged leadership team with strong expectations of what to do with data-summary deliverables, like executive-summary presentations, board decks, or readouts. The leaders here don't sit around waiting for overviews every quarter; they pore through the individual deal reports because they want to know the nitty-gritty details. They often actively contribute to discussions around program design and learning objectives. I have plenty of clients where the CEO is actively involved, sitting in on every bi-weekly research update call.

Action-oriented win-loss programs begin with an outcome in mind then collect data toward satisfying that outcome. The data will be used as a basis for decision making—often as validation for a decision, not the only source of truth. Once all the inputs are collected, these programs drive change and support big decisions.

For instance, one of my first clients had a known gap within their solution, an order management system (OMS). Although the gap was known, the supporting data they needed to pull the trigger, and measure the severity of the problem, came from the research program. The CEO wanted to answer, "Are we losing clients because of that gap? Are we losing out to competitors because of it? How important is it?" Based in part on the data the program collected, the CEO realized this gap was indeed a big deal and the company needed to do something pretty quickly—in their case, acquire another company.

THE VERDICT

Level 4 is where the full potential of a win-loss program is realized. Driven by leadership, there is a structured approach to prioritizing and executing on actions, and actions resulting from the program at this level have a better chance of succeeding and a greater impact on the overall business.

---

1. What level is your program at today?

2. What value are you receiving based on the current level of your win-loss program?

3. What are you missing out on based on the current level of your program?

4. What stage do you want your organization to be at?

DO YOU SEE TREES...OR A FOREST?

No matter what level you're operating at, you have the potential to generate value for your business. But the closer you can get to Level 4, the better off you and your company will be.

That doesn't mean you need to take the express elevator and zoom straight up from the basement to the penthouse. Developing a win-loss program is a cumulative process. As you build your core program and add on necessary pieces, your program will gain momentum until everything is in place and you can drive action and change. You can start at Level 1 and build to a Level 4 program over time—but it doesn't just happen.

Just like it takes a while to earn a black belt in martial arts, it takes a while to reach a Level 4 win-loss program. Unlike with martial arts, however, this doesn't have to be a linear progression. You can skip levels—going straight from Level 2 to Level 4.

To get there, you need some key foundational elements:

- The right program-management structure in place.
- A bought-in leadership team that takes ownership of the program.
- A plan for reviewing the findings and building an action plan then executing that plan and measuring the impact.

If you're not at a Level 4 today (and you're likely not), I want you to see what's in front of you, not just so you can get excited about it, but also so you can use that knowledge as a way to socialize the opportunity to others within your organization, to get their buy-in.

To do that, I want you to see the forest for the trees. In this case, the forest is the grand opportunity in front of you, and the trees are the details of all the things that need to happen for you to get to the point of seeing the great benefits of a win-loss program. There's a game-changing opportunity for your company here if you put the time and energy into doing this right.

Now that you have a better understanding of where your own win-loss program is on the spectrum and the potential that lies ahead of you, it's time to take the first step toward building a win-loss program that works for you: getting buy-in from the right people in the right way.

ACTIONS & TAKEAWAYS

1. Your competitors likely have a win-loss program of their own. You're either catching up or pulling ahead.

2. Evaluate your program to determine if it is Sales-Sourced, Siloed, Integrated, or Action-Oriented using the chapter's criteria.

3. Identify which departments and individuals are involved in your program to gauge whether it is siloed or cross-functional.

4. Review your data-collection methods to check if they are informal or structured, as structured methods indicate higher maturity.

5. Assess the level of leadership engagement in your program, as active involvement signals a more mature program.

6. Measure if insights lead to specific, measurable actions, as high actionability indicates a mature program.

CHAPTER 3

Getting Your Stakeholders in the Game

IMAGINE YOU'RE GIVING A KICKASS WIN-LOSS READOUT PRESEN-tation to your leadership team.

Leading a top-down, Level 4 program (just like I laid out last chapter), you're feeling quite confident about the results you're about to deliver. As you look around the room, you notice all the playmakers are in the house—and you know their minds are about to be blown by a presentation chock-full of awesome and actionable insights for each of them.

Over the next several minutes, you deliver a compelling account of your buyer's journey, complete with a set of key opportunities and recommendations to catapult your organization to the next level.

Following your presentation, you ask each leader to return to their respective teams, deliver your findings, and create a prioritized action plan to address each opportunity. They comply. When you reconvene, each team shares the same feedback: the win-loss research provided such a detailed account of what their buyers want it was almost like those buyers were sitting in the room with them. With the robust intelligence you delivered, they saw clearly how they could evolve their thinking, prioritize their efforts, and take immediate action.

Feels pretty good, right?

As I discussed last chapter, your win-loss program can generate a small, compartmentalized impact at any stage of the Maturity Model. However, if you're working at a Level 3 or above—engaging and collaborating with stakeholders across the organization—you have the opportunity to make more meaningful and impactful change on a much larger scale. Working at this level, when it comes time for your quarterly, biannual, or annual meetings, you get to be the rock star who gifts all these stakeholders with the information they need to move the company forward.

That's the end goal, anyway. But to make that happen, you have to start at the beginning: getting your stakeholders bought into the vision of your win-loss program. If you skip this critical step, your chances of succeeding are significantly lower, no matter how well you've designed the program. In this chapter, I'm going to share the major stakeholder groups throughout your organization who will benefit most from your win-loss program. Then, in the next chapter, I'll show you how to engage with those groups and generate buy-in by creating a shared set of learning objectives.

THIS IS A GROUP EFFORT

You've probably heard of the hub-and-spoke model. This model can be applied to many different fields, from business operations to sharing intelligence. In the case of a win-loss program, your hub represents your organizational priorities, and the spokes represent the individual priorities of the different functional groups within your company. The work each of these functional groups (spokes) performs each and every day contributes to the company's overall objectives (the hub).

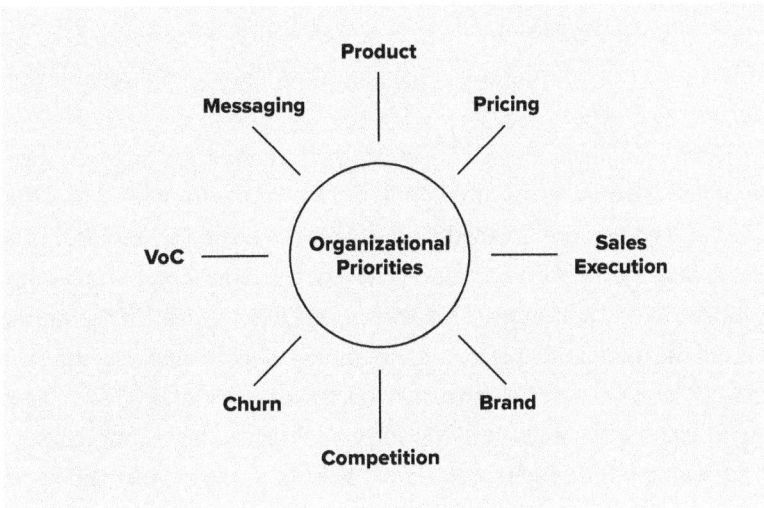

Figure 3.1

Your job, as the owner of the win-loss program, is to understand who the different stakeholders are at the ends of those spokes, identify how they may benefit from your program, and get them involved in your program-design process as early as possible.

To make your win-loss program a true shared effort, you need to make it real for them. On every spoke in every department, your stakeholders are trying to get a better picture of a specific part of the buyer's journey. The better you understand what they might want to know upfront, the better you'll be at delivering meaningful insights.

So, let's get started! In the following sections, we'll take a look at some of the specific stakeholder groups in your organization and how they might benefit from a win-loss program.

THE CEO

Senior leaders love win-loss programs because they offer a birds-eye view into deal dynamics that is otherwise invisible to these executives. Leadership rarely gets a boots-on-the-ground view of why they're winning or losing deals—which means their single version of the truth is limited to whatever the salesperson believes happened. As discussed in the past couple chapters, that's not a very reliable version of the truth.

Here's the challenge. CEOs know their perspective of what's happening in the business is often limited. They'd love to check under the hood and get a more detailed look at how the engine's running, but a few slides on win-loss trends during quarterly business review meetings seldom satisfy their hunger for knowledge. They yearn for the *stories* behind the numbers, a better understanding of what they're doing well and not so well in addition to answers to key questions, such as how their buyers feel about their offering compared to their competitors.

A well-executed win-loss report is bullshit-free—just the facts served straight up so the CEO can understand the buyer's true perspective. It's the deep, detailed insight they crave. If you're able to get your CEO engaged in your program, you can bet they'll read each word of every report you produce and regularly reference your findings during staff meetings, making you an indispensable asset and your program a strategic C-level resource!

I know this because I see it happen all the time. One of my former clients, for instance, was a software company that later sold for $1.8 billion. Its CEO read *every* word of *every* twenty-page win-loss report sent to his inbox because he wanted to understand what was happening out in the field. This was his opportunity to be a fly on the wall and keep his finger on the pulse of sales, performance, market perception, competition, and product feedback, all in one place. Time and time again, he told me he had a million other things to read, but he chose to read the win-loss reports because they were the best source of information about what was going on within his business.

PRODUCT MARKETING

Let's move on to your team: product marketing! As you probably understand by now, win-loss programs are often run by product marketers. Whether the team conducts the win-loss research themselves using internal resources or leverages a third-party win-loss provider, such as Klue, win-loss program ownership often lands in your court.

As you can imagine, win-loss insights are extremely important to product marketers, as these insights help you effectively position your organization's products and services in the market. By capturing regular intelligence from buyers who have just evaluated your offering and that of the competition, product marketers are better equipped to make smarter, more informed, GTM decisions, improving their chances of positive outcomes.

The program enables product marketers to stay on top of shifting market conditions and buyer preferences on an ongoing basis by providing answers to important questions.

- Are buyers changing?
- Are their needs changing?
- Are competitors' GTM efforts changing?
- What do we need to do so we're not standing still and getting run over?

As a product marketer, you know being several steps ahead of your competitors may make the difference between winning and losing. A win-loss program can help you better understand what's happening in the field and how to improve your approach in a number of ways, including:

- Improving GTM messaging and materials.
- Determining which events or communities to participate in.
- Training salespeople how to effectively communicate differentiated value-proposition messages out into the marketplace.
- Anticipating and preparing to address key objections or concerns buyers might have related to your solution or the competition.

The better you can answer needs and questions like these, the better you can align your messaging to your ideal customer profile. This in turn means generating more qualified leads and more valuable information to feed to your salespeople.

SALES LEADERSHIP

Next, we have sales leadership. This group wants to beat the competition more often, close more deals overall, make more money, and qualify to attend their company's annual President's Club trip on some tropical island far away. In order to do that, they need to find ways to get ahead and improve overall team performance.

Win-loss interviews alone provide sales leadership with the tool they need to coach individual salespeople on their performance. It's like holding up a mirror so the salesperson can clearly see how they appear to the buyer, identify what they're doing well, and understand where they could improve. Ultimately, win-loss interviews enable sales leadership to tell salespeople what to keep doing (bright spots) and what to rethink about their approach.

Can this be a tricky proposition? Absolutely. Sales tends to attract overconfident types who regularly claim they know every single little detail about each deal in which they are involved. (Ask me how I know. I have been a salesperson for over twenty-five years in one way, shape, or form.) Not to beat a dead horse, but this overconfidence often clouds their sense of why they truly won or lost a deal. My research regularly shows that salespeople's perceptions are often quite off-base, if not outright wrong. Without conducting a win-loss interview and sharing the results with sales, it can be tricky to convince them their views may not be accurate.

At the same time, salespeople are also leery of someone else sniffing around their deals. The primary reason for this attitude is not all sales processes are picture perfect (shocker!). Just because a deal was won does not mean the sales process went well or the salesperson even knows why they won the deal. (In my earlier years as a salesperson, I can distinctly remember occasions where contracts were miraculously signed without warning. I was always pleasantly surprised, of course, but rarely asked why since I didn't want to look a gift horse in the mouth.)

So yes, for salespeople, there's often some pride standing in the way of meaningful improvement. But at the end of the day, salespeople really do want to become better at their jobs. They just aren't sure how to take that next step—and they can be a little defensive when others suggest changes to their approach.

This is why win-loss research really is in their best interests. It provides them with an honest, objective perspective of their performance and allows them to better understand what their buyers want and how to serve them. Not only does a win-loss program help them close their perception gap, it also equips them with invaluable nuggets of intelligence, like building blocks, they can use to be more effective, close more deals, and make more commission dollars!

At the end of the day, sales leadership—and your entire organization for that matter—wants salespeople who are both confident and capable. Win-loss programs don't just help individual salespeople identify areas for improvement, they also help sales leaders identify systemic issues that affect the entire team.

A rising tide lifts all boats. Individual coaching may lead to a higher win rate for that salesperson—but a team of salespeople who *all* have higher win rates translates to more closed deals, more revenue, and more commissions!

SALES ENABLEMENT

If you're in charge of sales enablement, strong win-loss data gives you real insight into how your team is performing—both what they're doing well and what they're not doing so well.

- Is your team slacking on their executive presentations?
- Do salespeople stumble over themselves trying to explain pricing and packaging?
- Is your sales team offering crazy discounts that make no sense and put off buyers?
- Is your team as a whole coming off as a bunch of used-car salespeople?

Instead of guessing at what you need to improve, with a win-loss program, you can objectively identify where your team needs to tighten up. The analysis of win-loss data can help you identify macro-level trends about salesforce effectiveness, offering you big-picture insights into where the team needs additional resources and training.

For instance, through their win-loss program, one of my clients was able to identify significant variability in their discounting practices, which was leading them to not only lose deals but also leave money on the table. Once they had this feedback, the sales-enablement team was able to quickly respond. They built a more structured approach to discounting and a tighter ability to communicate the reasons for discounting, which ultimately helped improve their win, renewal, and retention rates, increasing the company's revenue.

Win-loss interviews help sales enablement in a few specific areas. The first is new-hire onboarding. Sharing a selection of win-loss reports is a great way to introduce new hires to your buyers, their needs, and your sales process. By carefully selecting a set of reports, sales enablement can imprint ideas and best practices into the minds of new hires when they're most open to input.

The second area is ongoing training, recognition, and empowerment. By sharing win-loss reports with the sales team on a regular basis, you are able to show them what's working and what's not. Whether on an individual or team level, training should be based on what your buyers are saying, not what any one internal person believes the team needs. Receiving this feedback directly from the buyer has more impact for salespeople motivated to hit numbers and earn commissions; they are being told exactly how to do that from the people actually on the other side of the deals.

I've been a salesperson, a sales manager, and a sales VP (manager of managers). When I was a salesperson, I didn't always agree with my manager's feedback—especially when it felt biased or subjective. In turn, when I became a sales manager, I sensed some of my team didn't agree with the feedback I was giving them. When I became a sales VP, it was even harder. Win-loss reports address this challenge by providing insights into the true gaps in training and reasons deals are not closed in a way that reduces any bias or subjectivity. It's hard for a salesperson to disagree when presented with the buyer's own account. When all parties agree on what needs improvement, you can quickly put a plan in place to work together on a solution.

COMPETITIVE INTELLIGENCE

Win-loss programs generate a ton of amazing competitive insight that may be leveraged in a number of ways to stay ahead of the competition.

Competitive intelligence, or competitive enablement, means not just collecting data but turning that information into a tool kit to be used during the sales process to differentiate yourself from the competition and position your offering against other offerings available in the market.

Here's what it comes down to: the more intelligence you have, the more you can build out your battle cards. In case you're unfamiliar with the term, battle cards are live documents or flat files that include all kinds of intelligence about competitors.

- How are they pricing their solution?
- How can we position ourselves against them?
- What are they saying?
- What is the latest news about them?
- What's significant about their executive team?

The better you can answer these questions—and the more accurate your answers—the better your responses will be when talking to potential buyers.

Win-loss programs can also help your competitive-intelligence team through improved training. Competitive-intelligence teams often run regular new-hire and sales-enablement training sessions. During those sessions, they provide an overview of the competitive landscape and updates on competitive movement. Fresh intelligence on competitive positioning—where your company is winning and losing—and competitor pricing can make those training sessions that much richer and more compelling.

Finally, competitive intelligence is regularly called upon during senior-leadership or board-level meetings. Their insights support important and costly decisions related to development, hiring, and GTM strategy.

PRODUCT MANAGEMENT

Any organization that has a product wants to know how that product measures up. This is doubly true for B2B technology companies. Whatever they're selling, product managers want to know:

- Does our solution resonate with the marketplace?
- Does it have the right capabilities?
- Are we providing the right experience through our platform?
- Do we have the right integrations with other technology platforms?
- Are we secure enough?
- Are we fast enough?
- Is our uptime an issue?
- Do we need international capabilities?

And that's just for starters. Every product manager I've ever known has an endless list of questions—and win-loss programs are a great way for them to get those answers. Not only do win-loss programs provide product managers with invaluable insights regarding their buyer's preferences and priorities, they also help them better understand how their solution stacks up against competitors in key areas.

Through a win-loss program, the product-management team can validate their roadmap, ensure they're on the right track to identify future opportunities based on future needs, and explore partnerships, acquisitions, and development efforts.

One of my clients, who runs a conversation intelligence platform, initially reached out because they had reached an inflection point. Given the state of the market and where they were with their product, they could go one of two directions. The problem was they had no idea which direction was the right one. Their win-loss program helped them better understand what their buyers wanted relative to what they offered. This gave the product-management team the insight they needed to pivot their product roadmap successfully.

CUSTOMER SUCCESS

Customer success, the people responsible for managing and renewing existing accounts, may not seem like a traditional choice to care about win-loss programs. After all, customer success is all about client *retention*. Why should they care about why some deals are won and some lost?

It's true that win-loss programs are primarily concerned with the beginning of a relationship—where the buyer has either chosen to work with your company or not. However, many win-loss programs include churn analysis as well. Sure, it's important to understand why you first won a client, but if you lose that client a year or so later, you're going to want to know why that client decided to move on.

When you think about it, churn is simply another win-loss point with a twist: here, *you're* the "incumbent solution" the buyer is moving away from. From the perspective of customer success, this can lead to a bajillion questions—all of which a win-loss program can help answer.

- Was there a problem with the onboarding process?
- Did they not get the right support?
- Did their needs change?
- Did our solution not align with their needs to begin with?
- Did they have a bad customer-management experience?
- Did we make a change to our offering that didn't align with their use case?
- What are all the reasons it didn't work out?

Often, the client has considered their experience with you and found it lacking. But that's not always the case. It could be the client decided to bring their effort in-house. Or it could be the business is going in a new direction and no longer needs your services.

Whatever the case, the customer-success team is going to want to know about it—which is why they have a huge stake in a successful win-loss program.

DON'T FORGET THE OTHER BIG WINNERS

Your internal stakeholders aren't the only ones to benefit from a win-loss program. There are two other big groups that also stand to benefit quite a bit: buyers and investors.

The buyers should go without saying. After all, the information you're collecting will ultimately make their lives better. The more you take the feedback to heart (and make positive changes), the better their buying experience becomes. Maybe you'll learn your salespeople need to listen more and sell less. Or maybe you'll learn your pricing model is so confusing it makes buyers uneasy. Whatever you learn, if you make adjustments to your approach, you're improving your ability to connect with customers and prospects.

You probably didn't think of your investors though, did you? We work with many venture capital and private equity firms in support of their portfolio companies, so we often hear firsthand how much investors appreciate a well-informed founder or executive team. Coming equipped to board meetings with a detailed account of deals and thorough understanding of buyers and competitors inspires confidence in investors that their investee is well-informed and on top of things!

ARM YOURSELF WITH KNOWLEDGE

These are the biggest stakeholders in your organization who stand to benefit from a win-loss program. But at the end of the day, you'd be hard pressed to find a team or individual within your organization that wouldn't find value in each deep, detailed account of a buyer's evaluation experience.

In order to be a good advocate for your win-loss program, you need to understand how the whole organization benefits. While what I have shared provides a preview into the potential use case of each group, I do recommend reaching out to the team lead for each group to discuss what type of information they may be interested in and how you may be able to serve their needs through your win-loss program.

Armed with this knowledge, you can create advocacy and build the buy-in your win-loss program needs to be successful.

ACTIONS & TAKEAWAYS

1. A win-loss program without stakeholder and leadership buy-in is dead on arrival.

2. Every stakeholder group has something to gain from the insights produced by a win-loss program. Your job is to understand those potential benefits as you work to get their endorsement of or participation in your program.

CHAPTER 4

Laying the Foundation

THERE'S NOTHING WORSE THAN SHOWING UP TO A MEETING AND presenting data to people who just don't have the context to understand its value.

You know why you're there (to present awesome, mind-blowing insights that will help the company grow exponentially), but *they* have no idea why they're there. They were simply invited to a meeting and told to show up. They may or may not know who you are and are likely quite skeptical of what you're presenting.

And the worst part? They may not share your enthusiasm for the insights you're about to present and the wisdom you're about to impart.

So, you get up there, passionately present your findings, and even make a few compelling recommendations to the group. Afterward, you think to yourself, "Crushed it."

As you wrap up, you ask if anyone has any questions.

"I have a question," says a very-senior-level-looking person at the head of the table. "Why in the world should we believe you, an outsider without our intimate understanding of the business? Our business is very complex!"

Have you ever let go of an untied, fully inflated balloon and watched it zip around the room before tumbling to the floor? That's about how you feel right now.

Ask me how I know.

This story isn't some hypothetical. It's exactly what happened when my team and I presented a big client's win-loss findings after months of working on their program. Only this didn't just happen once with this client. In the span of two weeks, we presented the findings to several different teams within that company, none of which we had any previous contact with. Each group had the same response to our presentation.

- "I think I know my business pretty well. Your findings don't match up."
- "We have to take this with a grain of salt. After all, the sample size is too small."
- "Why am I just hearing about this program for the first time? Who determined which questions to ask and who we should interview?"

Freakin' *brutal*.

It should come as no surprise to learn that account did not renew.

But why? What happened? As I said, this was a big client with many different products and divisions. Our research program was designed to cover all those product areas, each of which had their own divisional leadership.

That's all pretty normal, but here's where things went sideways. Despite the fact that our program had the potential to impact so many different areas of the company, we were granted no access to a single leader or stakeholder during the design phase and research period. We did great work, but without including those leaders in the planning process—and the buy-in that collaboration would have generated—the executive summary readouts were, to put it lightly, a flop. All those months of effort were effectively wasted.

This is why I'm spending so much of the early part of this book not on the technical how-tos of starting a successful win-loss program but rather with a set of human-to-human how-tos. Mark my words, if you skip the step of asking for stakeholder input during the program-design phase, my story could just as easily be yours.

So, who are you stakeholders? They're your internal customers, the people you're building this program for in the first place. You know, the people we just spent all of last chapter (which you definitely read) talking about. But this program shouldn't be some top-secret gift you're surprising them with. You want them to know what you're building, appreciate the value of your win-loss program, and bless the effort. At the end of the day, if you're not selling your win-loss program internally and engaging your stakeholder group from the start, it's going to be difficult to get people engaged once you start to share results. And, of course, if no one's interested in what you're doing, they're far less likely to benefit from the insights you're generating.

So, let's dive in. For the rest of this chapter, I'm going to teach you how to use the discovery and goal-setting process to generate buy-in and advocacy for your win-loss program. By focusing conversations on key learning objectives, you'll not only create a sense of ownership among your stakeholders, you'll also have a much clearer sense of the most pressing organizational needs your win-loss program can help address.

START WITH LEARNING OBJECTIVES

As you set up the foundation of your win-loss program, your goals are twofold: establish a key set of learning objectives, and get buy-in for your program from key stakeholders. These goals are intertwined. By putting an early emphasis on learning objectives and enlisting stakeholders to help build those objectives, you also generate the awareness of and buy-in for your program you've been looking for.

So, what are learning objectives? Simply put, they're a way to make sure you're not running your win-loss program blind. Most win-loss programs have little direction and aren't tied to any organizational or departmental goals or initiatives. The program manager might be collecting valuable data, but there's no plan for how to deploy that data to reach the program's true potential.

This is like going to a restaurant without a menu. You show up, the staff brings out five random dishes for you to eat, and you have zero say in the matter. If you're lucky, you're in the mood for one or two of those dishes. You could even end up having the best meal of your life! More likely than not, however, you're going to walk away disappointed (and probably still a little hungry).

When you've established a clear set of learning objectives for your win-loss program, on the other hand, it's much more like the kind of restaurant experience you're used to. You look at the menu, see all the possible paths you could take, and then carefully and intentionally select what you'd like for your beverage, appetizer, entree, and dessert. Your order informs the specific actions the kitchen will take to cook and deliver that delicious meal to you.

Now, let's put this in business terms. What are you in the mood for? What would you like to learn in your win-loss program?

You might already have an idea of what you're looking for, but here's the thing: you're not just ordering for yourself. You're ordering for the whole table—that is, your internal stakeholder group and likely your leadership team. Knowing that, it's probably a good idea to check in with everybody before you order. What information do they need to uncover through the program, and how do their needs align with the company's overall objectives? The better you can answer these questions, the happier everyone's going to be when they get served a plateful of fresh, personalized win-loss data (and the more you're going to look like an absolute hero).

Individual, departmental, or organizational learning objectives come in all shapes and sizes. Like the client we discussed in Chapter 2, they might want to collect pricing feedback from buyers so they can get the budget to hire a pricing manager. Or they might have broader learning objectives. For instance, sales leadership might want to know how the sales team is performing. Are they helping the company win deals or lose them? Are they part of the problem or the solution?

These broader objectives can lead to surprising results. For instance, sales leadership might learn that their sales team is pleasant, responsive, and professional but that they have a tough time explaining their pricing model or how their solution is different from their main competitor's. If sales leadership can train their team on each area, they'll improve their overall close rate—increasing revenue and market share in the process.

These are just a couple examples. Once you've identified your objectives, you can begin mapping out the path to achieve them. But first, you have to get out there and start talking to your stakeholders about what you, and they, want. In the next section, I'll identify the most important stakeholders to talk to—and discuss how to get them to buy into your win-loss program.

GENERATING BUY-IN

When you give the key stakeholders in your program a say, they develop a sense of ownership in the program. Instead of wondering why they're being called in to watch a stranger present findings that make very little sense to them, they'll show up eager to see what insights you were able to turn up with the objectives they identified at the beginning of the program.

Then, when you're presenting to them, you can say something like, "Hey, Judy, remember those questions you had about sales execution? Here's the data," or "Hey, Mark, this analysis answers your question about pricing. Turns out you were right: we *do* need to simplify our pricing model." From your initial conversations, you're now able to connect all the dots with your stakeholders and make them feel like this program was designed for them personally—which, in a sense, it was.

Hopefully, you're starting to see the forest for the trees here: when you talk to your stakeholders, you get them excited about what they can learn and how that information will help them drive results. When you skip this step, you're handicapping your program's success from the start.

Before you get to this ideal state of personalized (and appreciated) insights, you need to know who to talk to. Whose support do you need to make this program work? Who stands to gain the most, look the best, and become the largest and most influential program advocates?

When it comes down to it, there are three big groups of stakeholders you need to focus on: C-level executives, functional leadership, and sales. Let's look at each of these groups one by one.

C-LEVEL EXECUTIVES

As discussed in Chapter 2, one of the characteristics of a Level 4 win-loss program is a top-down commitment to the program. It makes sense, then, that you'll want to start generating both learning objectives and buy-in at the tippy top.

Buy-in at this level is an especially big deal since it means securing not only the approval to launch your win-loss program but also the time and other resources necessary to conduct it. However, to make your program run, the executives in the C-suite must understand the value they're going to get from backing your program.

In case you're worried about how these conversations might go, don't overthink it. It could be as simple as the following:

You: Do you feel like you have a good sense of why we're winning and losing deals and what we need to do to win more and lose less?

CEO: Not as good a sense as I'd like.

You: What if I told you I could help fill in the gaps?

CEO: I'm listening.

You: I'm interested in launching a win-loss program where I would interview our buyers to find out why they selected us over our competition.

CEO: Sounds interesting!

You: Aside from win-loss reasons, I could dig into other areas—business drivers, selection criteria, product, pricing, sales experience, you name it. I could analyze all the data and present my findings to you and your leadership team on a monthly basis. I just need your endorsement and thirty minutes of your time to help shape the program priorities.

CEO Yes. Of course!

Pretty straightforward, right? No complex machinations, no bending and twisting their arms to say yes to the program. Just lead with the value they're likely to get. Make it personal. If they're worried about competing priorities, make it clear this isn't a heavy lift—just an upgrade to an existing process. That way, it'll look like a no-brainer.

If you can get C-suite buy-in, it's like getting a celebrity brand ambassador to endorse your super-cool t-shirt line. Once you have that endorsement, you can reference it over and over again to gain buy-in from the next group of stakeholders: functional leadership. Better yet, have the CEO reach out to let them know it's an important initiative and everyone should support you in every way they can.

FUNCTIONAL LEADERSHIP

Leadership tends to be about results, results, and more results. They're busy executing on a lot of different fronts, and they're not going to waste time discussing a win-loss program if they don't think it will help them achieve their objectives faster.

To engage with leadership, make your intentions clear. Invite them to be a part of the program-design process. Ask them directly for their input. I recommend sending a short, five-minute survey that asks each member of the leadership team three core questions:

1. What are you looking to learn through our win-loss program?

2. What three questions would you personally ask buyers if you were the interviewer?

3. What specific actions will you take with the findings to support your goals?

The idea behind the first question is to get leadership to lean into the program through collaboration. You want them to feel like their voice was heard and their objective recorded and included in the program-design process.

The second question gives you a more specific sense of each leader's interests and blindspots. The head of sales, for instance, may want a better idea not only of why they're winning or losing deals but also how their sales team is performing. Meanwhile, the head of product might want to know how people feel about the product, the product's key strengths and weaknesses, and where they should be investing their engineering resources to keep pace with the needs of their ideal customer profile.

The third question is important because these programs tend to fizzle out when nobody does anything with the data. In order to have an effective program, you have to take actions with the data collected. And in order to have control over those actions, you want to get a sense upfront from stakeholders: what *is* the plan of action for that data?

As you can see, these stakeholder interviews are part data gathering, part program promotion, and part insurance policy; if the results you produce aren't what they expected, you can simply point back to your discovery process as a way to remind them what their objectives were at the start of the program and what they had planned to do with the data.

Once you've gathered this information from each leader, you can start to look for overlap. For instance, you may discover nearly every single person on the leadership team wants to learn more about the competition. If that's the case, you've not only identified a key cross-functional interest area but also a priority learning objective for your program.

With your aggregated and prioritized learning objectives in hand, the next thing to do is socialize them. Share back what you've discovered with the members of the leadership team, ideally in a group-meeting setting. Confirm the learning objectives align with the group's overall research goals. They should. After all, the objectives are *their* objectives! The more aligned leadership feels with your program and the learning objectives, the more likely they are to buy into the program.

ASK YOURSELF

1. Do you feel you have the support of senior leadership?

2. Are they as excited about the program as you are?

3. Do you have a good sense of their individual and collective learning objectives?

SALES

The sales team can be your biggest supporter or the greatest barrier to your win-loss program's success. When the sales team hears that product marketing is building out a win-loss program, the first thing most on the team think is, "Oh shit, this is going to be all about deal inspection and micromanagement! *How do I get out of this?*"

Sure, there could be a component of that—if sales *is* blowing deals, it's in the company's best interest to know why. But that's not the spirit of the program. Far from it.

The spirit of a win-loss program is to help drive organizational change and make improvements to benefit the greater good—especially sales. Your job is to help sales understand this is *not* a witch hunt, their perspective matters, and they'll have direct input into program design.

Your goal isn't to criticize or place blame on sales but to gather super valuable data to determine where the company collectively needs to invest and improve. If your organization is able to do that successfully, the positive results will most likely be felt in sales more than any other team.

You know that. The C-suite knows that. Functional leadership knows that. Now, you just have to make sure your sales team knows that. Not just so they won't torpedo your program, but also so they will provide warm introductions to all their buyers so you can conduct your win-loss interviews.

To get the sales team's buy-in, start with the head of sales. Just like with all the functional leaders, your goal is to ask for their feedback. What do they want to learn about their sales team's effectiveness? What are your competitors' sales teams doing differently? What knowledge gaps do they suspect the sales team might have?

These initial discovery conversations will go a long way in securing sales leadership buy-in. Then, once you start conducting interviews and delivering win-loss reports, the sales leaders will be eager to review each report, knowing they provided important input and helped shape the program. From there, they'll be more than happy to embrace and endorse the program to their sales team.

To get sales leadership on your side, here are some best practices I recommend:

- **Be transparent.** A critical component of a successful win-loss program is not to build and run the program behind the sales team's back but with their input and buy-in. Without them, you will lose the opportunity to make the program stick.
- **Highlight leadership's endorsement.** If sales leaders endorse the program, sellers themselves have no choice but to participate. Ask

leadership to mention the program on a regular basis and hold their team accountable for cooperating.

- **Be clear on the burden.** There's no doubt about it, sellers are busy people! However, make it clear you're not asking much of them, just the minimal effort required to qualify buyers into the program and help connect you with those buyers.
- **Clearly communicate the benefits.** A 2014 Gartner study found that organizations that engage in formal win-loss programs see a significantly higher close rate and larger average deals than those that do not.[2] There are many reasons for why this happens, one of which is the fact that win-loss programs often resurrect no-decision or dormant deals that were perceived lost. Whatever the case, the point is if you craft your message around the benefits to sales specifically, they'll get pumped. After all, sellers are always interested in hearing how they might put more money in their pockets.
- **Remove the perception of any threat.** Emphasize that the program will not just look at sales execution but also competition, product, pricing, and other key business drivers or selection criteria. The less they think the program is designed to make them look bad, the better!

We've all been in situations where a project is being launched and we have to calculate the ultimate survival rate of the effort with the amount of time we're willing to commit. When sharing your plans with stakeholders, make sure they understand this is not just another fly-by-night experiment. If you can make this clear—and if you can give them some agency in establishing the learning objectives—they will be far less likely to be fearful or critical of the program.

---

2   Bob Apollo. "Gartner: 'Boost Your Sales Win Rates by 50% Via Win-Loss Analysis." *Yahoo! News.* May 20, 2014. https://www.yahoo.com/news/gartner-boost-sales-win-rates-50-via-win-133103162.html.

In preparation for your stakeholder interviews, email each stakeholder to set expectations. Use the email as a way to collect some initial input to help you prepare for the actual discussion. Here's an example:

Bob,

Thanks for agreeing to meet next week for thirty minutes. As you know, I'm working to upgrade our win-loss program (yay)! I'm going through the initial planning process now. As one of my primary internal customers, your input is super important. I want to ensure that as we start conducting buyer interviews, we're collecting information that will ultimately help you achieve your personal and team objectives. In preparation for our meeting, would you please complete and email me the following statement.

If I knew_____, then I could _____, which would result in _____.

Thanks!

(You)

This simple-yet-effective exercise will help you better understand what knowledge the stakeholder yearns for, what actions they would be able to take if they had that knowledge, and what results they would expect to see as a result of actions being taken based on that knowledge.

By taking this step, you're putting yourself in an awesome position to deliver a valuable, well-aligned, and action-oriented win-loss program. In addition, because you collected this information up front and subsequently delivered value, you're going to solidify the importance and impact of your win-loss program.

DISCOVERY

Now that you've gone to your key stakeholders, generated buy-in, and established your key learning objectives, you're ready for discovery. All great win-loss programs begin with solid internal and external discovery processes. This is your chance to better understand both the state of your business and any external factors about your buyer or market you may not have been aware of. Let's take a closer look at what the internal and external discovery processes involve.

INTERNAL DISCOVERY

As a product marketer, when was the last time you took a comprehensive look at your company's sales process, end to end? When was the last time you reviewed your product team's ideation and road-mapping process?

Here is your chance to refresh your understanding of how different groups within your business operate. For instance, if you want to know more about the sales team, you might listen to a handful of recorded sales calls to hear how your company positions its solution compared to key competitors.

What you hear, or don't hear, might surprise you. A product feature you thought was a huge differentiator, for example, might not even come up on the call. Or you may notice the salesperson struggles to clearly articulate your pricing model.

Whatever the case, the point isn't to correct anything you see or otherwise try to improve approaches and processes. The point is to learn about your company, cast away any outdated assumptions you might have, and step into the shoes of different team members so you can better understand their current thinking and approach.

If you notice potential areas for improvement, go ahead and make a note of them. These will be hot topics to explore in your win-loss interviews.

EXTERNAL DISCOVERY

On the external side, your primary goal is to look at your competitors. How are they perceived in the marketplace? How do they position their offerings?

More than likely, you'll have some of this competitive intelligence already. This is your chance to update that intelligence and further build out your learning objectives and interview priorities.

Believe it or not, a well-executed external discovery process can be a huge factor in increasing your chances of beating key competitors. For example, if you read on social feedback platforms, such as Reddit or G2, that Competitor X has poor customer support and doesn't respond quickly to requests, you can leverage that topic in your buyer interviews by asking questions like, "How important is support to you?" or "How did our company compare with other vendors evaluated in the area of support?" Without this external discovery, you may not prioritize these questions—missing out on key learning opportunities as a result.

To understand how your competitors are positioning their services, differentiating themselves, and managing their reputation, here are some sources to try:

- **Your sales team.** Ask what they're hearing about your competitors. It's all but certain they've heard at least something non-public and can provide some interesting insight.
- **Competitor websites.** Remember, your competitors do exist out there in the real world. Don't be afraid to poke around and see what you can learn about them. After all, one of the primary goals of a win-loss program is to collect as much information about your competition as possible. To ensure you're as prepared as possible, check out the following pages on your competitions' respective websites:
  - **News.** All sorts of announcements live here, such as new product or partnership announcements, information on leadership changes, or even earnings reports.
  - **Events.** What events are your competitors attending, sponsoring, or presenting at? Are you also attending these events? Can you get your hands on their presentations?
  - **Product pages.** Here, you'll get a great idea of your competitors'

offerings to compare with your own capabilities and identify key differences.

- Customer case studies. You can bet that people you're selling to have checked out your customer case studies as well as those of your competitors. Taking the time to view what they've viewed will put you in a stronger position as an interviewer.
- Career page. Job postings can provide a ton of interesting insight into your competitors' operations.

- **Social media.** It is important to review the same social feedback sources your buyers likely reviewed during their evaluation process. If you fielded an online survey as part of your win-loss program (see Chapter 5) and a buyer shared that they looked at Reddit and read some reviews of your offerings and you found those reviews to be negative, you'll be better prepared for that topic when it comes up.

- **Interest-based communities.** Today, many buyers are part of some form of online or offline community. The community may be based on role, industry, or interest area. If you're not familiar with your buyers' communities, ask around, starting with existing customers. Joining these communities will give you insight into chatter regarding your company and competitors. Keep in mind these communities are designed for sharing, not lead sourcing. Be careful not to do any selling within the community—or you run the risk of being banned!

- **Peer-review sites.** Sites like G2, TrustRadius, and even Glassdoor give great insight into a company's inner workings, sales motion, and client experience.

- **Analyst research.** Gartner Magic Quadrant and the Forrester Wave Report tend to be the standards, but keep looking. You'll be surprised at what you might turn up. This is another great way to put yourself in your buyers' shoes since there is a very good chance the buyer you're interviewing has also reviewed those reports, read each vendor description, and developed certain assumptions and biases either for or against your company.

At the end of the day, your goal is to get as much comprehensive knowledge as you can to learn what you're already doing and what your competitors are doing. Build out your landscape in every direction so when you come into these conversations, you have the context and background to lead a kickass interview. And if you're having trouble managing all this data, here's some good news: companies like Klue offer platforms to help you automatically collect, organize, and distribute competitive data at scale, saving you a ton of time.

BUILD YOUR MAP—THEN ACT

At this point, you have input and buy-in from your key stakeholders, and you have your agreed upon learning objectives. This early work is going to be essential in the long-term success of your program. Be careful here. While you've put in a lot of good work up to this point, all that hard work won't amount to much if you don't act.

Aside from establishing your learning objectives, it's also important to create a vision for how you will use your data and how you will measure its impact. What are your objectives, and what actions will you and your stakeholders take once all that fresh, piping-hot data is served up?

When I was just starting out in win-loss, my very first client shared something obvious, yet profound. "We previously worked with this other win-loss provider," he said. "But nobody really cared about the data. It ended up just sitting on a shelf, collecting dust!"

That's the moment I recognized what had been right in front of me all along: you can have the best win-loss data in the world, but all that information is useless if it isn't packaged in a way that drives actions that lead to measurable results. Yes, in order to build a successful win-loss program, you need to establish the initial learning objectives. But you also need to think through how to operationalize, distribute, and act upon the insights.

This extra step can be accomplished while you're interviewing stakeholders and establishing learning objectives. All it takes is an extra question or two.

For instance, if your sales manager says, "I want to know how my sales team is performing," don't let the conversation stop there.

Instead, follow up on that statement. "Okay, we're going to get you those answers," you might say, "but what are you going to do with that data?"

If they come back with a statement like, "Well, I don't know," be prepared to help by brainstorming some options. For instance, you could ask one of the following:

- "How do you see this data contributing to your quarterly business reviews or annual sales kickoff meeting?"
- "What about weaving this data into new-hire training or one-on-one sales coaching conversations?"
- "How would you use this data to help build the business case for budget requests related to new sales tools?"

As you can see from these questions, you and your department heads have tons of potential ways to leverage your win-loss findings. While whatever path you choose should be specific to both your team and your needs, it should also be action oriented. At a minimum, your sales manager should commit to reviewing the data and identifying areas of opportunity. From there, they could meet with their sales-enablement leaders and build a plan for getting the right resources in-house to help fill the gaps in their sales motion. Finally—and here's the big part—they could determine how they're going to track their progress to determine whether the changes they're making help improve their win rate, exceed revenue goals, or shorten the sales cycle.

Does your sales manager have to commit to these actions at this stage? Hell no. They're free to change their mind down the road all they want. In fact, they likely won't know what the appropriate actions should be until the data is in their hands. The point of this conversation is to get that manager engaged with the program and thinking about how they might choose to use the data.

Fair warning: these can be uncomfortable conversations. Imagine going through the drive-thru and asking for a cheeseburger only for the person on the other end of the intercom to say, "Well, why do you want a cheeseburger? What are you going to do with it? How will it improve things for you?"

Umm...awkward, especially when you're hangry. "Just give me my damn cheeseburger," you yell back at the box. "The freakin' impact is that I'll be less hungry!"

You may receive a similar reaction, especially from the leaders who never asked for a win-loss program in the first place. But it's important to train all stakeholders to think about the outcomes—not just what they want to learn but how to take that knowledge and successfully apply it to improve outcomes for the entire organization.

DO IT ALL...OR YOUR PROGRAM WILL BE DOA

When it comes to planning and designing your win-loss program, the steps outlined in this chapter couldn't be more important to your overall success. But while program managers don't often skip this step, they typically don't knock it out of the park either.

It's not enough to get in front of the CMO, CPO, or the CRO and ask for their opinion. That's too limited a conversation to get any useful information, and it's unlikely you'll get them even thinking about your win-loss program, let alone get them bought in. Surface-level conversations get surface-level results. The deeper you go here, the better off you'll be down the road.

Remember, your big goal is to get your stakeholders to fully lean into your program, embrace it, and feel some sense of ownership of it—to get them excited about the reports coming out and the actions being taken. The quickest way to do that is by including stakeholders in the design process and making them feel like their opinion matters—a lot.

As you move through this initial discovery process, remember this is not a one-and-done activity. Plan to reassess your program learning objectives at least quarterly. The market and your competitors are constantly changing, after all, and your program learning objectives must be adaptable and agile to change with them.

Once you have everyone on board and you know what your stakeholders are looking for, you can all work toward a common set of goals. From here, there's just one question: how, exactly, do you plan on collecting all that juicy information? In the next part of this book, we're going to take a deep dive into the interview-planning process.

ACTIONS & TAKEAWAYS

1. Win-loss data presented without context isn't helpful. It's confusing. Sometimes, it might even be seen as threatening.

2. Once you know who your stakeholder groups are, begin recruiting each target stakeholder into your program. Pay extra attention to sales leaders. Of all stakeholder groups, these are often the people hardest to win over.

3. Once you've brought your stakeholders into the program, work with them to establish clear, actionable learning objectives.

4. Don't stop at learning objectives. Before conducting your first win-loss interview, make sure you and your organization have a plan to operationalize, distribute, and act upon the insights.

PART 2

Nailing Your Interview Guide

CHAPTER 5

Setting the Foundation

WE ALL KNOW THAT THERE ARE GREAT INTERVIEWS, GOOD INTER-views, and, well, not-so-good interviews.

On the not-so-good front, imagine showing up to your first win-loss interview with no set plan. You've done zero prep, are working from a generic set of interview questions, and have no clear plan of attack. Sure, you've never done this before, but how bad could it be?

With unearned confidence, you sit down at your desk, dial into the call, and hope for the best:

"Hey, what's your role?"

"Where are you from?"

"What does your company do?"

Ugh. Talk about unimpressive.

In this scenario, beginner's confidence may keep you from realizing it, but your inexperience is showing. In fact, it's radiating off you. Your interviewee is floored—and offended—by your lack of preparation. They know, as you do, that you could have at least spent two minutes on LinkedIn prior to the call to gather the answers to those basic, lame questions. No win-loss interviewer has ever built any sense of rapport by asking for basic biographical data.

An unprepared interviewer is an ineffective interviewer. If you're just winging it, you'll be much less likely to connect with the person you're interviewing—and without that connection, you have virtually no chance of capturing research lightning in a bottle. Maybe you'll get a useful data point here and there, but those golden nuggets of insight that help you validate and grow your win-loss program will evade you.

Delegating the work is unlikely to go any better. Just because a salesperson knows how to ask good questions doesn't mean they'll make for a good win-loss interviewer. In fact, in my experience, sellers' interview questions are often more cringe-worthy than those of the unprepared interviewer. Sure, the seller might at least know the interviewee's name, company, and role, but they're less interested in exploring the buyer's experience and much more interested in pulling the deal from the ashes and breathing new life into it.

As a result of that single-minded focus, these are the kinds of questions your seller is likely to ask:

"So, tell me, why didn't you choose us?"

"What if we were to drop the price by 20 percent?"

"What can I do to change your mind?"

As you can see, with a seller at the helm, you've gone from a *win-loss* interview to a *win-back* interview. This might suit the seller just fine, but there's a cost—chiefly, all that precious win-loss data you wanted to collect to inform your stakeholders and fulfill your learning objectives.

If either of these scenarios reflects your approach to win-loss interviews, then what's the point?

A poorly designed and executed win-loss interview helps no one. Sure, you'll get *some* information, but you won't satisfy your learning objectives—which was the whole point of this program in the first place.

However, when you put some thought into how you design and conduct an interview, engineering it in such a way that it supports your learning objectives for the program, that interview will lead to more fruitful outcomes and better intelligence that can be used internally to drive change and improve win rates.

Preparation and design are critical to a successful interview process. Here, in Part 2, I'm going to take a deep dive into design and preparation, walking you step by step through the key components of an effective interview so you arrive at every call ready to connect, learn, and grow. Think of Part 2 as your own personal playbook of best practices, packed full of valuable insights gained from running win-loss programs for over ten years and hundreds of companies.

To kick things off, this chapter is all about the big picture of interview design and how the information you're collecting fits into your broader learning objectives. After all, there are multiple pieces to this puzzle, so it's important to know what you're building toward.

THE MOUNTAIN RANGE

A successful win-loss interview begins with a well-structured plan for collecting data. Here, there are three components at play:

1. Well-defined learning objectives.

2. An online survey designed to capture higher-level directional data points.

3. A smart interview guide designed to cover your primary learning objectives with the ability to probe into areas of priority.

To understand how these components work together, think of a mountain range. Each individual mountain represents one of the key learning objectives you built with your stakeholders through the discovery process (remember that from the last chapter?). The larger the mountain, the higher priority the objective.

On the top of each mountain is a snowcap, representing the data you can collect through a simple online survey. The questions and answers are typically higher-level, and the data collected is limited. The online survey can be used the same way many surveys are: to cast a wide net across a broad group of won or lost opportunities. In support of an interview, the online survey can also be used as a way to collect intel from someone who has agreed to an interview. By sending the survey link as pre-work in preparation for the interview itself, not only will you get to the good stuff quicker during your interview, you will also arrive at the conversation better prepared.

Finally, the base of each mountain represents the data that can be collected through your interviews. As with real mountains, the area below the snowcap is the widest and deepest. The information that comes from an interview is just that: deep and wide. You'll also notice that, at the base of the mountains, the mountains merge together and form valleys. The valleys represent the organic nature of win-loss interviews. While survey questions are often siloed, interview questions and their answers can transcend learning objectives.

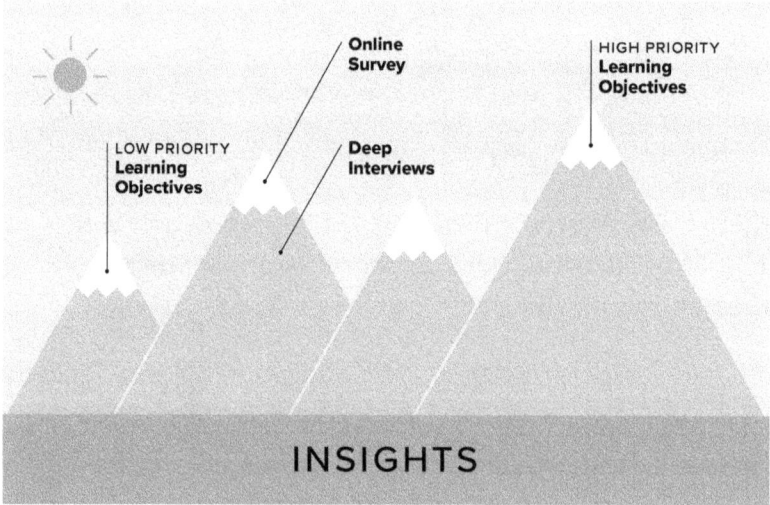

Figure 5.1

In this mountain-range model, the data from across online surveys and interviews comes together to produce qualitative and quantitative insights to help support the key learning objectives for your team.

When I share this model with product marketers or other business leaders, I often get the same question: if interviews produce the greatest amount of depth, why bother producing and distributing an online survey? Simple: you can't interview everyone. Even if it were possible, it wouldn't be worthwhile.

If your company cycles through a thousand opportunities a quarter, there's *no way* you're going to interview all one thousand buyers—even if each was willing and able to speak with you. Forget about it. Most companies only have time to interview ten or twenty buyers per month. Typically, they down-select deals that are high-value, have strategic significance, or exhibit some other key criteria, such as losses to a specific competitor (I'll talk more about how to identify key interview targets in Part 3.)

Of course, after selecting your top ten to twenty deals, you still have about 980 to 990 other deals you could look at. That's where a well-designed online survey comes in handy. Ask the deals you're not targeting for interviews to complete a short survey. Beware, however, that (1) response rates are often low with surveys, (2) the data is less reliable than the data from an interview, and (3) analyzing the quantitative data may present challenges given the small sample you're likely to receive across unique segments such as region, industry, or company size.

The other big benefit of this two-pronged approach is it gives you the best of both worlds in terms of collecting quantitative and qualitative data. Some people love quantitative data, with all the beautiful statistics, trends, and graphics you can produce with it. Survey responses lend themselves nicely to data visualization. Interviews, on the other hand, are largely unstructured, *qualitative* data made up of a series of great quotes and stories. By combining the two, you get a much more complete view of not only *what* happened with your deals but *why*.

Now that you understand the basics of the mountain-range model and how it works, let's take a closer look at each area.

People always ask, "Which do I write first, my interview questions or my survey?"

The interview guide and the online survey are typically created at the same time; they just serve different purposes. One is a conversation guide—in other words, the things we want to talk about. The other is more pointed, measurable data we can use to identify trends over time or trends we want to explore further through interviews.

We've collected all this information through the discovery process. Now, we're ready to use that information to write the questions within the interview guide and the survey in parallel.

START HERE: LEARNING OBJECTIVES

When your company is cycling through a thousand opportunities a quarter, how do you choose the ten or twenty opportunities you ought to prioritize for interviews?

The way a lot of companies make this determination—and, just so we're totally clear, we try to get people *not* to do this—is to look only at the deals that are super exciting: "We lost this big deal, and the executive team wants to know what happened." You may be able to capture a solid anecdotal story from that one deal, but it's not going to help you conduct a meaningful trend analysis.

It's like asking, "Why did you break up with me? What did I do?"

Well, if you ask one ex-partner and their answer is, "I dumped you because I love tennis and you don't play it," that's a hell of a story!

However, if you had a series of short-term relationships and you learned from each that they dumped you because you prioritized time with your friends and left them with nothing to do on a Saturday night, that's a more meaningful trend to work with! This example demonstrates the difference between a one-off (bias toward tennis) and trend analysis (friends over lovers). Both yield interesting information, but the latter paints a much more comprehensive—and actionable—picture of the problem.

Instead of looking only at the super exciting deals, look at deals that fit certain criteria, may serve to validate a hypothesis, or answer a specific question. I call this group of deals a "research cohort." This is explored in more detail in Chapter 18, but the basic aim is to collect data from a set of deals that share three core characteristics—such as deal size, location, industry, competitor, or product/service type. At the end of the day, you want to be able to tell a story, and in order to do so, you need to have related pockets of research.

For now, this basically means holding a deal up to your learning objectives and saying, "Okay, it checks off four of our five objectives. That's worth an interview."

Are you beginning to see the method here? Again, nobody has time to interview everyone. Focusing on your learning objectives helps to narrow your focus and determine who you will be prioritizing—and who you won't.

DESIGN YOUR INTERVIEW GUIDE

Once you've determined *who* you'll be interviewing, you'll want to know *what* to ask during that interview. It may seem obvious, but it's a good idea to write out your questions and create an interview guide you can have in front of you during the interview process to keep you honest and ensure you're touching on all the key areas you need to cover before you hang up the phone.

There are two types of questions to consider including in your interview guide: outcome-first and action-oriented questions.

OUTCOME-FIRST QUESTIONS

Outcome-first questions help ensure your questions align with your learning objectives. For example, let's say during the discovery process, the top three questions your stakeholders identified were:

1. How is the sales team performing?

2. What are people saying about our competition?

3. How do people feel about our offering?

Questions like these speak directly to the current state of your organization. You're not focused on doing anything with this information yet. You just want to understand how your operation is producing the results it is. Build your interview guide around these outcome-first questions, with a section around each learning objective. Within each of those sections, write three or four open-ended questions that inform that learning objective.

ACTION-ORIENTED QUESTIONS

Next are your action-oriented questions. Remember, the best win-loss programs don't just lead to interesting insights. They lead to direct actions that can benefit your business in a number of ways. That's why, during the discovery process, it's important to ask stakeholders not only what questions they want answered but what actions they plan to take with the data.

Action-oriented questions give your interviewee the opportunity to weigh in on what those actions could look like. For example, imagine your CEO is looking to leverage your win-loss program to narrow in on a set of actions that will lead to greater results. Knowing this, you may include a question such as, "If you were the CEO of Company X, where would you invest in the business and why?" Based on the responses to that question, as well as other inputs from the business, the CEO can take immediate and measurable action.

By building your interview guide in this way, you're able to create a sticky program that adds immediate and broad value across your organization.

When designing your interview guide, here are three helpful tips to remember:

1. **Write twenty to thirty questions.** You might only end up asking ten to fifteen of these during the actual interview, but you'll be prepared no matter which direction the conversation goes.

2. **Keep the call to thirty minutes (but block out an hour).** For most people, a half hour is just enough time to get important insights without pissing anyone off. Sometimes, however, your interviewee will have more to say—especially if the conversation is going really well. So, be sure to block off a full hour on your calendar just in case your interviewee wants to continue.

3. **Keep your questions clear, concise, and open-ended.** Stay away from complex or multi-part questions. It's important your interviewee understands what you're asking and is able to answer without having to twist their brains trying to remember all the pieces to your questions. (I'll show you more about how to do this in the upcoming chapters of Part 3.)

DON'T SKIP THE ONLINE SURVEY

Don't tell anyone's mother I said this, but not everybody is worth interviewing. If your company performs several transactions every month or quarter, there's simply not enough time to interview every-body—and, quite frankly, there's no reason to interview everybody anyway.

That said, just because somebody isn't worth getting on the phone doesn't mean they're unimportant. In fact, they're most likely a prime candidate for an online survey.

You probably already know how to do this. Just pull up your favorite marketing-automation tool, create a template email, add your survey link, send it out to all recent closed opportunities, and see what you get back. Boom. Just like that, you've collected a bunch of quantitative (and possibly qualitative, if you've feathered in some essay-style questions) data from the opportunities you decided not to interview.

The survey portion also allows you to look at a different dimension of the data. While a well-designed survey should only take about seven minutes to complete, you can capture eighty to a hundred different data points through smart question design. For example, you might ask the respondent to score your product across eight key areas. Within the same question, you might ask the respondent to also rate each area by importance. That one question generates sixteen unique and useful data points!

Please rate the following criteria by importance and your view of our capabilities

	IMPORTANCE					YOUR COMPANY				
	1	2	3	4	5	1	2	3	4	5
Analytics & Reporting	○	○	○	○	○	○	○	○	○	○
Ease of Integration	○	○	○	○	○	○	○	○	○	○
Usability	○	○	○	○	○	○	○	○	○	○
Multilingual	○	○	○	○	○	○	○	○	○	○
SSO	○	○	○	○	○	○	○	○	○	○

Figure 5.2

Finally, the online survey is also a great way for the interviewer to capture initial feedback prior to each live interview. The best interviews are the ones you're most prepared for, and one of the best ways to prepare is to start learning directly from the interviewee ahead of time. If built properly, the online survey will collect a lot of interesting detail about the buyer's evaluation journey and act almost as a cheat code for the interview itself, touching on many of the same areas the interview will but at a more tactical level. In other words, not only do you get some valuable initial data, you start to get a sense of where to go with the conversation to unlock the good stuff.

As an example, your online survey might ask the interviewee to score your product or service in certain key areas. If you notice a particularly positive or negative score, you can bring it up in the interview: "Hey, I noticed you scored us really low in the area around usability. Can we talk about that?" Just like that, the survey unearthed an important data point you were then able to dive deep into during the interview.

It's that kind of one-two punch that makes the online survey such a valuable part of the mountain-range model. Rather than going in blind and not knowing what you might uncover, you call into every interview with your eyes wide open and ready to dive into some of the interesting responses to survey questions—all but guaranteeing the interview is that much more fruitful.

That said, the online survey isn't a mandatory ingredient to a successful interview. It's just nice to have. If the interviewee doesn't get the survey back to you before the interview, you'll still be in good shape to conduct a high-value interview—as long as you completed all your other prep, of course.

SO MUCH TO ASK, SO LITTLE TIME

By now, you may find yourself wondering, "How can I possibly cover all this ground in a thirty-minute call or a seven-minute survey?"

Part of the answer to that question is that you will have to prioritize what is most important to you. So, before any interview, ask yourself, "If I had to walk away from the interview with the answer to only *five* questions, what would those questions be?"

Whatever those five questions are, make sure you've worked them into your interview guide.

As you're preparing your online survey, here are two tips to keep in mind:

1. **Create data cuts.** Design your survey in such a way that it collects a set of metadata that will allow you to slice and dice the data later. Metadata are simple data points, such as region, deal size, and product, that will enable you to sort data easily. You'll find that most metadata points can be gleaned from your CRM opportunity records. The more metadata points you collect, the more data scenarios you can explore. These scenarios are known as "data cuts." If, for example, your learning objective is to identify the difference in buying behaviors based on investment level, asking a question like, "What was your budget for this purchase?" will provide you with the ability to segment your data by deal size. From there, you may like to go deeper and look at the same data broken out by region. Without metadata, this is a nearly impossible task. With metadata, it's as easy as changing the filter on an excel spreadsheet.

2. **Keep it to seven minutes.** The amount of time it takes to complete a survey is more important than the actual amount of questions in the survey. Just like I've found a half hour to be the ideal phone interview time, I've found seven minutes to be the ideal online survey time. Any longer, and takers will start to get survey fatigue, which may affect the reliability of their responses. If you're not sure how long your survey takes to complete, take it yourself—or better yet, have some of your stakeholders take it.

Will you always get to ask those five questions? A lot of the time, but not always. We've all been in interviews that just go on and on, where the tough-to-corral interviewee talks (endlessly) about anything and everything that's on their mind. As you develop more skills as an interviewer, you'll learn how to interject and lead your interviews more effectively to ensure you check those five questions off your list.

That said, remember to record and transcribe all your interviews. This will not only catch things you may have missed, but as you'll see in Part 3, these recordings and transcriptions will come in handy as you're building out reports for the leadership team.

But first things first: asking the right questions for the right learning objectives to get you the right information to take the right actions. For the rest of Part 2, I'm going to teach you exactly how to do that, walking you step by step through all the potential categories of learning objectives so you'll always know what questions to ask and how to ask them.

Consider these next chapters a template you can adapt to fit your needs. You'll want to go deep on some of these topics, and others might not be as important to you. That said, since your win-loss program is likely to evolve and focus on new learning objectives as it matures, it's useful to see what each category is all about.

ACTIONS & TAKEAWAYS

1. No successful win-loss interview is conducted on the fly. Before conducting your first win-loss interview, build your "mountain range" with well-defined learning objectives, an online survey, and a smart interview guide.

2. Don't disguise an attempt to reel the buyer back into a sale as a win-loss interview. Yes, sometimes a win-loss interview can result in getting a deal back on track, but that should never be your goal.

3. Identify your key targets. Not all won or lost sales are worth interviewing. For those that aren't, focus on engaging them through an online survey instead.

4. As you design your interview guide, focus on two areas of questions: outcome-first and action-oriented.

CHAPTER 6

The Warm-Up and Persona

WE'VE NOW SPENT FIVE CHAPTERS SETTING YOU UP FOR SUCCESS as you prepare to conduct your very first win-loss interview. You understand how to justify a win-loss program, recruit key stakeholders, and conceive of the entire end-to-end process.

Now, only one question remains: how the heck do you get started?

First, it's important to understand the framework guiding your big-picture approach. Rather than jumping from one seemingly unrelated research topic to the next, your win-loss interview should follow a logical flow. That's right, you're going to bring your interviewee on a journey—one that starts when they realize they have a problem to solve and continues all the way through the decision they made to address it.

As a product marketer, you are likely already familiar with something called "the buyer's journey framework." This framework follows the buyer through three stages of the buying process: *awareness, consideration, decision*. Not only is this framework useful in your work as a product marketer, it's also useful in organizing your win-loss interview. In fact, a strong win-loss interview *should* map quite closely to the buyer's journey.

Tailoring your program begins with identifying what's most important

Win-Loss-Churn Research Opportunity Zones

Persona	Awareness	Consideration	Evaluation	Decision			Churn
Background	Drivers	Scope		Vendor Comparison		Decision	
Demographics	Internal Forces	Risk Assessment	Research Options	Brand & Reputation	Vision Match	Decision Factors	Churn Reasons
Experience	External Forces	Vision for Solution	Evaluation Process	Marketing Materials	Capabilities	Contract / Negotiation	Customer Lifecycle
Responsibility & Metrics		Education / Consensus	Committee	Differentiated Value Prop	Roadmap		Product Experience
Personal Goals		Business Criteria	Resources Leveraged	Perceived Benefits	Price		Support Experience
Challenges		Technical Criteria		Sales Experience	Partner Network		Advice
Reporting Structure		Business Case					

Figure 6.1

PRO TIP

Here's the very coverage map that we use to orient clients. Within, you'll notice the stages of the buyer's journey and the key research topics within each stage. You'll also notice additional areas such as Persona and Churn to illustrate that you're not confined to the stages of the buyer's journey but have the ability to go well beyond.

This chapter only focuses on the initial warm-up questions you'll be asking your interviewee. However, even those questions should be asked with some intentionality and awareness of the big-picture journey you'll be taking your interviewee on. For those reasons, let's take just a moment to explain the buyer's journey framework before moving on to your initial warm-up questions.

The first stage of the buyer's journey is awareness. In this stage, the buyer becomes aware of a problem they must solve. To understand that problem, during win-loss interviews, we tend to ask open-ended questions such as:

"When did you realize you had a problem you needed to solve?"

In the awareness stage, not only is a problem identified, initial actions are taken. To uncover these actions during interviews, we ask questions such as:

"What did you do next, and what did you do after that?"

By asking these questions, we're looking for the buyer to open up. For instance, in response to the previous question, they might say something like:

"I became aware I had a problem to solve, and as a result of that, I took the next steps, which were to talk to my boss and get budget approval."

Following the awareness stage, the buyer moves into the consideration stage. In this stage, they consider their options. The different solutions available to them may include something like upgrading their current system through homegrown development, looking at a third-party vendor, or working with a consultant.

Finally, the end-stage of their journey is reached when the buyer ultimately makes a decision; they decide to buy from you, buy from someone else, or buy from no one at all.

You'll see this journey reflected throughout the remaining chapters here in Part 2. Use this understanding of the buyer's journey to shape questions and guide your decision-making.

Of course, before you jump headfirst into the buyer's journey, it's always good to take a little time to get to know your interviewee and establish rapport. After all, you need to know the *hero* of the buyer's journey before you follow them on their quest. If you lead with the tough, awkward questions right out of the gate, they may shut down on you. For the rest of this chapter, we'll explore not only how to get the conversation rolling but also how to establish a rapport that leads to a deeper, more valuable discussion.

ALIGNING THE WARM-UP WITH YOUR LEARNING OBJECTIVES

A great way to ease anyone into a conversation is to get them to talk about a topic they know oh so well: themselves. Asking questions about them not only breaks the ice and warms them up, it also helps you start satisfying some basic learning objectives—chiefly, understanding the buyer persona.

Marketers in particular are eager to understand their buyers. The greater their understanding, the better they can tailor their message in a way that aligns with and attracts those buyers. As part of their process, product marketers will often build out *buyer personas*, which, according to my friend Adele Revella, founder of the Buyer Persona Institute, are "examples of archetypes of real buyers that allow marketers to craft strategies to promote products and services to the people who might buy them."[3]

To build out those personas, product marketers typically seek to understand their buyer in the following areas:

- What is their role within their organization?
- What is their experience?
- What are their core responsibilities?
- How is the person being measured (e.g., a salesperson is measured on activity and quota achievement)?

---

3   Adele Revella, *Buyer Personas: How to Gain Insight Into Your Customer's Expectations, Align Your Marketing Strategies, and Win More Business* (New York: Wiley, 2015).

- Who do they report to?
- What are some of their greatest challenges?
- What are their aspirations?

By answering these questions—and I'm simplifying here—a product marketer can begin to build out a detailed description of this particular persona, which they will then use to inform their GTM efforts.

As an example, let's look at tech giant Salesforce. According to Salesforce:[4]

> [They] treat personas as archetypes of [their] users, viewed through the lens of the cloud that they use. Salesforce personas are crafted through rigorous data collection (observations, interviews, surveys) and analysis. They're more than a simple title or role—they're based on real users' behaviors, attitudes, desires, capabilities, tools, and perspective on the product, all within the context of their needs.
>
> [Their] personas are based on the general tasks users perform in their roles, rather than focusing only on what they do in their Salesforce CRM. Why do [they] do this? Because the Salesforce platform is highly flexible and customizable. This means people at different organizations may carry out the same task using different Salesforce features or products, or even other systems. Good news—by asking about users' goals, motivations, and general tasks, [they] are able to get a fuller picture and find similarities between users across different companies.

You may not be able to learn everything you need to know about your ideal buyer in a win-loss interview, but the warm-up can produce a treasure trove of useful information directly from the actual buyers, who are happy to answer these softball questions as they ease into the discussion.

---

4   Salesforce, "Get Started with Personas," Trailhead, 2022, https://trailhead.salesforce.com/content/learn/modules/ux-personas-for-salesforce/get_started_with_personas.

THE INTERVIEW GUIDE

During the warm-up stage of a win-loss call, you never want to ask questions such as:

- "What did we do wrong?"
- "Have you already signed contracts with the other vendor?"
- "Do we still have a shot?"

This is the approach we often see salespeople take when conducting a post-mortem call, and you can't fault them for trying. However, let me be clear on this point: if you're asking questions like these, you're *not* engaged in a win-loss call. You're engaged in a desperate, burn-the-bridges, last-ditch-effort win-back call.

It will come as no surprise that I strongly discourage you from taking this approach. If you begin with questions like these, you're starting the interview off on the wrong foot—and it's a super hard place to recover from.

Another important point to consider: don't make the warm-up about you and your study. If you spend too much time introducing yourself and providing study context, (a) they may not care, and (b) you're sacrificing precious time the interviewee could use to talk about themselves and their buyer's journey. Always remember that time is never on your side during a win-loss interview, so be smart about how you use it.

Instead, your goal in designing the warm-up section of your interview guide is simple: get the interviewee to talk about themselves.

But again, ease into it. If you were on a first date, you wouldn't lead by asking, "How many partners have you had?" That's unexpected, a bit personal, and super uncomfortable.

So yes, make that warm-up all about the buyer. Consider sharing a few tidbits you learned about them during your interview prep to let them know you've come prepared. You might even start by saying something like, "Hey, I see you've been at Acme for ten years. That's a long time. What do you like about working there?" or simply, "I'd love to start by learning a bit about you. Can you share a bit about your role and responsibilities?"

This approach is likely not a revelation for many reading this book, as this is standard rapport building 101. The key point is you don't want to go right into the hard questions; you want to warm them up by getting them talking about themselves, maybe even crack a smile or two. Building that connection creates a level of comfort that leads to sharing, which comes in quite handy as you move to those deeper, more complex questions.

Remember, although this is a warm-up and you are easing them into the conversation, you're still collecting a ton of useful information from the get-go. With that said, while this rapport building is great, do it quickly. The more time you spend hearing about the interviewees' life story and summer plans, the less time you'll have to gather proper win-loss feedback!

THE ONLINE SURVEY

Interviews aren't the only place to warm up your buyers. Your online survey is another place to set the stage *before* they ever get on the phone with you.

Here, the best way to warm up your buyer is to acknowledge the elephant in the room: you're imposing on them—*especially* when it comes to the buyers with whom you plan to conduct a live interview as well.

So, start by recognizing that their time is valuable. Show them you appreciate that they are giving you some of their incredibly valuable time to provide feedback to you—because they don't have to. (And if you are giving an incentive for participation, you may also want to mention it here so they can see what's in it for them.)

From there, give your buyer a little bit of context about the survey—chiefly that any information they share will be considered confidential. Something like this ought to do: "Your answers are going to be used internally only for continuous improvement efforts, so please be as open and transparent as possible." This will help reassure them they can be honest with their responses.

Then, bring it back to the time commitment: "On average, this survey takes approximately seven minutes to complete, but please take as much time as you need. The accuracy of your responses is incredibly important to our ability to use the data in a constructive manner."

Ultimately, you want them to feel appreciated, informed, and comfortable going into the survey itself. If you set the stage properly, people are more likely to complete the entire survey and give more thoughtful responses.

With that out of the way, you can begin collecting some basic demographic information to help with your research efforts. Start with their name, title, and company and then dig into a handful of basic questions, such as:

- What country do you live in?
- Approximately how many people does your company employ?
- What industry is your company in?
- Is your organization public or private?

Smart interview prep helps build that all-important connection. Just as you asked the interviewee to complete an online survey prior to the interview and reviewed their responses, you should also take the time to research the buyers themselves. By doing the right homework ahead of time, at a minimum, you can ask them how the weather is in Albuquerque, and, if you're lucky, you may find a really strong connection point, such as a shared alma mater.

Because you have that information—before you even try to get them to start opening up and providing you with additional persona-building information—you might start off with an icebreaker like, "Hey, I heard that Syracuse is the snowiest place in the country. Is that true?" (Spoiler alert: It's not. According to the all-knowing internet, that distinction goes to Mount Rainier, Washington, which sees over 645 inches fall annually.) Connecting is important, but remember to keep it short so you can spend more time on the call objective—learning about their buyer's journey.

Each of those answers is a different data point you can use to slice and dice the data set. But without asking, you won't get these data points—or you'll have to go back and add it in manually later. Save yourself the time and headache and just ask the questions.

Part of the process here is thinking down the road: if you have one hundred responses to this survey, how is your team going to want to parse that data? Have you asked questions that will allow that to happen easily?

That way, if Joe Stakeholder says, "I want to look at this data by country and company size," or Mary Stakeholder (no relation to Joe) says, "I want to see the data by industry: healthcare versus retail," you'll be ready with the answers—making you look like a rockstar in the process. This is an often overlooked area, so it's important to be thoughtful about the demographic questions you're asking.

GO INTO YOUR INTERVIEWS INFORMED—AND
EXIT WITH INFORMATION THAT *MATTERS*

As you prep for the warm-up phase, both for your interview guide and your online survey, here are two things to keep in mind:

1. **Don't waste your time looking to the interviewee for answers to questions you can easily find on your own.** Yes, you are going to ask some softball questions to get the conversation rolling, but there's some strategy here. For the peripheral stuff—what college they went to, what city they live in—that's on you to research prior to the call. For things you can't research, such as questions more directly tied to their role within the company, get them talking.

2. **Don't spend all day with the warm-up.** Remember, you only have thirty minutes with them. The warm-up can only last so long. Especially during the live interview, collect your info, take your cues, and move on.

At the end of the day, the goal is to come into this conversation well prepared and walk out with useful information. It doesn't really matter how many kids or what kinds of dogs your buyer has (unless you're working more on the business-to-consumer (B2C) side). What matters is learning more about your buyer's biggest problems, the challenges they face every day, and how you can help improve their lives. Yes, you're breaking the ice here, but you can still be strategic with a small batch of targeted questions that can help you hone your buyer personas.

ACTIONS & TAKEAWAYS

1. The warm-up isn't just for chit-chat. You can collect vital information during this part of the conversation—and set the tone for a success-ful conversation to follow.

2. That said, don't spend too much time here. Get in, set expectations, get a couple bits of info, and then segue to the rest of the interview.

3. Don't use the warm-up to collect basic demographic data. That's a waste of call time. Use the online survey for that instead.

4. Ask yourself: "What are three good go-to warm-up questions?" Write them in the space below.

CHAPTER 7

Business Drivers

IN CONDUCTING WIN-LOSS INTERVIEWS, ONE OF MY CLIENTS found that, nine times out of ten, the primary reason buyers were evaluating their solution options and considering switching vendors was as a result of leadership change. They found that when new leaders were brought in from the outside, they often brought their own biases toward or against certain vendors and had a "we're going to do it my way" mentality.

Armed with this knowledge (or perhaps validating what they already suspected), that company can now take specific actions that may put them in a better position to win more of these deals in the future:

1. They can closely monitor leadership changes within their client and prospect companies (for example, by tracking when people change their LinkedIn profiles, through press releases, or creating a Slack channel for their team to share what they've learned by word of mouth).

2. They can research the new leaders to get a sense of their background, vendor preferences, and even personal interests.

3. They can immediately build rapport with new leaders by congratulating them on their new positions through a kind gesture, such as sending along a small and appropriate gift with a personal note.

Smart and strategic steps like these are only possible because the company first took the time to do the research to understand the primary business drivers leading their buyers to evaluate solutions in their space. As a result, they were able to act first, giving them a slight advantage and improving their odds of scoring a meeting with that new leader so they can make the case for their solution. In this chapter, you'll learn how to design your business-driver-specific interview and survey questions to give yourself that same advantage.

LEARNING OBJECTIVES

Behind each evaluation, we find business drivers: the primary reason a buyer is looking for a solution. As product marketers, it's our job to identify those drivers and align our messaging and GTM strategy accordingly. While there are many common business drivers, we tend to see them fall into two broad camps:

- **Internal.** Such as a new leader joining the organization and wanting to adopt a platform they already know and love, internal growth-related projects, system consolidation, manual process automation, and movement from an on-premises solution to a cloud-based solution.
- **External.** Such as a regulatory and compliance shift in their industry, a provider sunsetting a product, an acquisition, shifting customer demand, and local and global socioeconomic and environmental factors.

When conducting win-loss interviews, your goal is to understand what drove that buyer to go out and look for a solution to their problem—and why now? What is significant about this moment in time that made them identify a need and seek out a solution?

Again, the biggest beneficiaries of this information are GTM teams. The better these teams understand what's driving an organization's evaluation process, the better they can align their messaging and strike a chord with their buyers. In other words, if buyers typically come to them during a leadership or regulatory change, they'll want to know that and be prepared with the right message.

The product team also stands to gain by learning more about an organization's business drivers. For instance, if the buyer is having issues with the incumbent provider, your competitor, and needs better mobile capabilities or a global platform to meet the needs of their global customer base, that's invaluable information, enabling the product team to build a solution that better speaks to that buyer's need.

THE INTERVIEW GUIDE

When designing your interview guide to learn more about your buyer's business drivers, here are some typical open-ended questions to consider:

- What were the key business drivers that led to this evaluation?
- What problems were you looking to solve?
- What challenges was this problem causing?
- What measurable impact were those challenges having on the business?

As we discussed in Chapter 5, the best way to get the information you want is to be *clear* about what you want. Ask simple, clear, concise questions your buyer can easily understand. It's not about complexity or being clever. If you have to explain your question, you may need to rethink that question for future interviews. Additionally, keep the questions open-ended so you're able to hear the buyer's story in detail.

THE ONLINE SURVEY

The business drivers section is an important section of your interview guide or online survey, but it's also fairly straightforward. There's not much difference between what you would ask in an online survey and what you would ask on a call or in a live interview.

The question to ask here is, "What were the primary business drivers behind your evaluation?" Then leave space for them to write an essay-style answer rather than making it a traditional radio-button or dropdown-style survey question. For such an open-ended question, you don't want to limit their options. After all, they may very well come up with something you didn't expect or plan for.

This question is especially important to ask in the online survey because you might collect a survey response but *not* opt to interview that buyer. The survey may be your only opportunity to hear the answer in their words.

For those buyers you *do* plan on interviewing, you can use their survey answers to guide your discussion in the interview. For example, you might say, "I see your primary business driver was leadership change. That's interesting; tell me more about that." Or "Did the leader come from another organization and have a preference toward a certain solution?" Having this starting point gives you an opportunity to prepare and probe deeper.

GO WITH THE FLOW

You may receive some surprising answers when you ask about business drivers in your win-loss interview.

Somebody might say, "We're being acquired, and we needed to have X platform in place in order for the acquiring company to do their due diligence on us." Or, "We had a significant data breach, and a lot of sensitive customer data was compromised, so we needed to find a new cybersecurity solution to help make sure that doesn't happen again."

I've even heard someone say, "We used another platform that

didn't live up to our expectations and caused us a lot of financial harm. Actually, it almost bankrupted us. Now, we're looking for a new solution to solve that problem."

That's painful!

Additionally, discussions around business drivers can graduate into a use-case discussion. Somebody might say, "The business driver was that we were preparing to enter a new market our current application infrastructure could simply not support."

You would then ask, "What were you looking for that solution to do?"

They might say, "I was looking for the solution to handle foreign language and currency requirements associated with these new markets." Or, "Our current solutions are great for the North American market but would not be able to support Europe."

If that's the case, follow the discussion and dive deeper.

ACTIONS & TAKEAWAYS

1. One of the biggest internal business drivers for a company seeking new B2B solutions is a change in leadership. Externally, the biggest driver is a regulatory or compliance shift in the industry.

2. Of course, that's not always the case. Your primary goal with this portion of the interview is to learn precisely why your buyer considered you in the first place.

3. Allow your interviewee a lot of space to share here. Don't try to pigeonhole them or guide them to an answer. Their reasons for considering your solution will surprise you!

4. Ask yourself: "What are three open-ended questions related to my business that will help me understand my target buyer's business drivers?" Write your answers below.

CHAPTER 8

Scope and Selection Criteria

LET'S SAY YOUR KID HAS A BIRTHDAY TOMORROW. YOU FORGOT TO order the cake, and now it's too late. But somehow, you still need a cake by tomorrow.

That's the business driver, the problem to solve. Next, you'll need to determine the scope:

- It has to be a chocolate cake.
- It has to be Taylor Swift themed.
- It has to serve at least eight kids.
- It must be ready before the party at noon tomorrow.

Now that you've determined your scope, you'll have to determine the selection criteria—in other words, the details that help you narrow down your choices from the available options. After all, there are lots of chocolate cake options that can serve eight kids and be ready by tomorrow, so it's important you pick the one that best meets your needs. After some consideration, you come up with the following criteria:

- Has to be available within five miles of home.
- Baker needs to have a 4.5-star average review score or higher.

Based on your scope and selection criteria, you've narrowed it down to two bakeries. Next, you decide to use their websites as the tiebreaker:

- One looks old-fashioned and boring. Pass.
- The other has a ton of cake pictures and happy kids blowing out birthday candles. It even has a Taylor Swift cake!

Looks like you've got a winner.

This buyer's journey process is what you're hoping to learn from your buyer—except instead of cake, you're interested in what scope and selection criteria they used to pick (or not pick) your product or service. While the scope broadly defines the job to be done, the selection criteria help your buyer narrow down their long list of options into a short list to choose from. In this chapter, you'll learn how to determine your buyer's scope and selection criteria so you can have your cake and eat it too.

LEARNING OBJECTIVES

In simple terms, scope and selection criteria help you understand what your buyers are looking for in terms of a product's or solution's features, functions, and capabilities. Once you know that, you can compare their feedback against your own offerings to determine whether your solution offers everything they need—or whether it's time for your product team to update their roadmap to better align with your buyers' needs.

The more such information you can gather during your win-loss interviews, the better equipped your company will be to create a solution your buyers will actually want. Here, sample size is important. For instance, if only two shoppers out of thousands want coconut frosting with their cake, coconut frosting isn't a big priority. On the other hand, if a full half of your buyers want a nut-free option, that's a significant finding. Information like this will help your product-development team determine where to invest and how to prioritize those investments.

Scope and selection criteria also help your marketing and sales teams with your GTM messaging by identifying which features to highlight: "Hey, our cake is perfect for any kid at any party because it's nut-free." Once you've discovered what your buyers care about, marketing can leverage the heck out of that—just keep hitting those topics over and over again.

THE INTERVIEW GUIDE

If your interviewee completed the pre-interview survey you sent prior to the interview, you should already have some idea of the respondent's selection criteria. But if they didn't complete the survey, start with these important questions:

- When looking for a new solution, what were your top three must-have selection criteria?
- Which of those three was most important, and why?
- How well did we align with your criteria?

To begin to build a picture of their scope, start with these four questions:

- What was your vision for a solution? (If they need further prompting: What are you hoping for, and what does it look like? What will it do?)
- What impact will the solution have within your organization?
- What benefits are you hoping to gain through this solution?
- If you had to put a number on it, what measurable gain or ROI are you hoping to see through those benefits?

There are three primary types of selection criteria: company level, core technology level, and product feature–function level.

1. Buyers' selection criteria at the company level might be something like:
   a. "We want to work with a company that has a strong reputation."
   b. "We want to work with a company that has other customers like us."
   c. "We want to work with a company that is financially viable."
   d. "We want to work with a company that has a really cool culture."

2. On the core-technology level, criteria could be:
   a. "We want to work with a company that has strong security."
   b. "We want to work with a company that has an easy-to-use solution."
   c. "We want to work with a company that can integrate with our core systems."
   d. "We want to work with a company that has global capabilities."

3. Finally, there are product- or service-level criteria. As an example, for an e-commerce platform provider:
   a. "We want to work with a company that has strong checkout speeds."
   b. "We want to work with a company that has strong mobile capabilities."
   c. "We want to work with a company that has smart shopping-cart capabilities."
   d. "We want to work with a company that has strong foreign language capabilities."

From the answers to these questions, you'll be able to build a pretty detailed buyer-specific use case. What you may find is there is not one use case for your solution but many. To illustrate that point, here are some examples of what your buyers might share:

- "We're using this to improve our accounts payable and receivable process because our current system is not able to scale into new markets."
- "We're replacing our core enterprise resource planning (ERP) system. We needed another accounts payable platform that would integrate with the ERP, and yours happened to do that."

See? Same solution, maybe even same industry, but totally different use cases. That's good to know.

From there, you can ask about selection criteria: "What were some must-haves within that solution?"

Finally, don't forget to follow up with the catch-all: "What considerations were most important to you when evaluating different options?"

In a thirty-minute interview, you won't be able to hit all the selection criteria. To save time, look for the highs and lows. For example, a buyer might rate global capabilities very low. When asked, they might say, "We're just local to North America. We don't have any plans to expand globally." And that answers that—you're not trying to get them to change their business model or market philosophy; you just want to know why they prioritize or deprioritize certain things.

But you also want to know if there's a disconnect. If you're marketing a feature you think is a huge selling point, but you're consistently finding no one gives a damn about it, your company will want to make some adjustments. These interviews give you insight into how well your solution delivers what your buyers actually want.

THE ONLINE SURVEY

In the online survey, the first question to ask is: "What were your top-three must-have selection criteria when you were looking for a new solution?" Then, give them three boxes to type in their answers. Avoid the dropdown list if you can. It's too leading. And besides, it's better to get these qualitative answers straight from the horse's mouth, in their own words.

From there, ask them to rate how well the company delivered in the three areas of selection criteria mentioned earlier:

- Please score the company's attributes in these areas on a scale of 1 to 5 by how important they were during your evaluation process.
- Please score the core technology in these areas on a scale of 1 to 5 by how important they were during your evaluation process.
- Please score the product features and functions in these areas on a scale of 1 to 5 by how important they were during your evaluation process.

Next, you'll want to learn what's most important to your buyers about the companies they're looking to align with. First, ask: "On a scale of 1 to 5, how important are the following attributes when partnering with a company?" Then, provide a list of options, such as:

- Reputation
- Financial viability
- Culture
- Years in business

Then, giving them the same set of options, ask: "How do you rank our company in each of these areas?"

These questions about company attributes help provide some really interesting insight into how the buyer feels about your company and whether that feeling was a positive or negative factor during their evaluation experience.

BE PREPARED FOR SURPRISES

Looking at selection criteria often invites surprises. What you perceive as one of your biggest strengths might turn out to be a weakness in your buyers' eyes.

For example, I once worked with a cybersecurity client whose key GTM message was that their founder was a member of his country's equivalent to America's CIA, and the rest of the leadership team were also all former intelligence officers.

The client was certain this was a strong selling point. They were wrong. When conducting our win-loss interviews with buyers, we consistently got feedback like this:

> We didn't see that as an advantage at all and were really looking to work with a North American company. It also made me a bit uncomfortable because they were pushing it so hard. If the founder worked for our own CIA or FBI, that may have been a different story.

That piece of feedback changed the course of how their organization went to market. As proud as they were that their leadership team served in these high-ranking military positions, their message was backfiring here in North America. The good news? Because they took the time to build out their win-loss program, they were able to bring this insight to the surface and quickly act on it.

ACTIONS & TAKEAWAYS

1. A buyer's business driver is the reason they decide they need a certain product or service.

2. The scope and selection criteria help the buyer narrow the field of potential solutions by defining specific parameters that must be met.

3. Scope and selection criteria are invaluable information for product designers and product marketers, allowing them to better understand what features their buyers value.

4. The more information you can collect, the better. But be prepared for surprises. For instance, it may turn out your buyers hate what you thought was one of your strongest selling points.

5. Think of three open-ended questions related to your business that will help you understand your target buyer's scope and selection criteria, and write them below.

CHAPTER 9

Product Feedback

WHAT IS IT ABOUT YOUR PRODUCT THAT HAS YOUR BUYERS OVER the moon?

What feature, function, or aspect of your offering was so great your buyers saw you as the obvious choice?

Don't know? Then don't skip this part of the research effort.

Product feedback is a huge area of opportunity within a win-loss program. While the selection-criteria portion focuses more on what buyers want out of a solution or vendor, product feedback focuses on whether or not a specific product actually brought the goods. Do your buyers see your product as innovative and cutting-edge or as something stuck in the eighties? Here's your chance to find out.

LEARNING OBJECTIVES

Why is product feedback so important to your company? At the end of the day, it means the difference between winning and losing business. If you lost a deal or two because of some sort of *misperception* about one of your products, you're going to want to know about it!

Naturally, product feedback is great info for product marketers.

Not only do you get a ton of intelligence on how to position your solution against your competitors, you also get to provide the product leadership team with critical insight to help them validate or inform their product roadmap.

THE INTERVIEW GUIDE

When seeking product feedback, there are two primary buckets of information.

COMMON PRODUCT FEEDBACK

Common product feedback is akin to asking someone for general thoughts on the city they live in. "How do you like Boston? Do you think it's safe? What's the restaurant scene like?" Replace Boston with Austin, and the same questions apply. Common product questions are questions that can apply to most offerings, especially in the B2B technology space. They will give you a sense of the general sentiment buyers have about your solution across common areas, such as ease of use, uptime, and ability to integrate. Whether you're selling a $100 million ERP to a fortune-class manufacturer or $100-per-month design software to a solopreneur, these broad topics and the associated questions are transferable.

- How did our product align with your vision for a solution?
- What did you like most/least about our product?
- How did the product compare to other products evaluated?

SPECIFIC PRODUCT FEEDBACK

The second bucket is specific to the solution being evaluated and the problems it solves. Specific questions are not transferable from one product segment to the next. As an example, if the solution was an e-commerce platform, you might ask:

- How did you feel about the mobile check-out capabilities?
- How did you feel about the customer navigation experience?
- How did you feel about the platform's page-design templates?

Asking those questions to a buyer that evaluated a cybersecurity solution would make no sense at all. Often, when asking specific questions, you're not just trying to learn about the buyer's perception of the current product features, you're also exploring what features your buyers might want in the future. Maybe they want more out-of-the-box web-page templates as part of the solution. Maybe they want to allow customers to process returns or easily join their loyalty program. Whatever the case, the more you can learn here, the more focused your product-development team can be in creating the next iteration of your product or service.

THE ONLINE SURVEY

The product-feedback portion of the online survey can be designed to capture both the importance of each common or specific area and the buyer's perception of your capabilities in those areas. In the survey, ask, "Please score the following areas by importance and your perception of our product capabilities in that area." If you're able, design a side-by-side survey question that includes two columns for feedback: one for importance, and the other for the buyer's perception of your capabilities (see Figure 9.1).

The following image provides an example of how you might design a "common product areas" question and another that covers "specific product areas."

Please rate the following product capabilities by importance and personal opinion of the capabilities of [Your Company]

	IMPORTANCE					YOUR COMPANY				
	1	2	3	4	5	1	2	3	4	5
Mobile Capabilities	O	O	O	O	O	O	O	O	O	O
Advanced AI	O	O	O	O	O	O	O	O	O	O
CRM Integration	O	O	O	O	O	O	O	O	O	O
Multi-factor Auth	O	O	O	O	O	O	O	O	O	O
User Provisioning	O	O	O	O	O	O	O	O	O	O

Figure 9.1

	IMPORTANCE					YOUR COMPANY				
	1	2	3	4	5	1	2	3	4	5
A Capability	O	O	O	O	O	O	O	O	O	O
B Capability	O	O	O	O	O	O	O	O	O	O
C Capability	O	O	O	O	O	O	O	O	O	O
D Capability	O	O	O	O	O	O	O	O	O	O
E Capability	O	O	O	O	O	O	O	O	O	O
F Capability	O	O	O	O	O	O	O	O	O	O
G Capability	O	O	O	O	O	O	O	O	O	O

Figure 9.2

The questions should be designed to not only collect product feedback but also identify the greatest disparities between what is important to a buyer and how they score each offering. By identifying the largest gaps, you're in a great position to ask second- and third-level probing questions in those areas during a phone interview.

Here's a big word of caution for this portion of your online survey: don't go overboard. You could easily create a whole survey just on product feedback. Don't. Just ask a handful of smartly designed questions that are aligned closely to what you care most about.

If you know you have kick-ass mobile capabilities and everybody else knows it too, don't include it here. You don't want to have somebody answer a question you're 100 percent sure about because that data is not going to add any incremental value. If you've rolled out a new feature recently and want some feedback, however, here is your chance.

For instance, if you learn a buyer rated mobile capabilities a 5 in importance but a 2 in perception of your capabilities, during the phone interview, you get to ask why. "I see that mobile capabilities are important to you, but you gave us a low score in this area. What led to that low score?" This is a great example of how survey data can steer the interview to enable you to hear the story behind the score.

FIND THE STORY

As you're collecting your product feedback, don't be surprised if you discover some sharp contrasts or contradictions. These are often the places where you can learn the most. If several buyers rate mobile capabilities as a key selection criterion but rate your particular solution as lacking, there's most likely a story there.

Exactly what that story is, who knows?

Maybe your mobile capabilities really aren't all they're cracked up to be. Maybe your sales team isn't really well-versed in your mobile capabilities and therefore is struggling to educate your buyers. Maybe your buyers are just flat out unaware that your mobile capabilities even exist!

Spoiler alert: online survey data can be very misleading. Respondents might not quite understand the question, they might be distracted, or they might be experiencing survey fatigue. That's why the interview portion of your win-loss program is so important!

There are a lot of different reasons gaps might exist between buyers' scores for product-area importance and your product's capabilities. Later, once you've sorted and analyzed your data, you'll have all the pieces you need to put that story together. For now, your job is simply to collect the data.

ACTIONS & TAKEAWAYS

1. Product feedback is another way to understand what your buyers do and don't like about your offering—this time from a first-hand user experience.

2. When seeking product feedback, divide your efforts into two categories: common product feedback and specific product feedback. This will help your organization understand how its product is received on the market in both a general sense relative to its industry and a targeted sense relative to its exact product.

3. The online survey is useful here, allowing you to get specific, quantitative data before diving deeper into feedback areas during the interview.

4. Think of three open-ended questions related to your business that will help you understand your target buyer's product feedback, and write them below.

CHAPTER 10

Pricing and Packaging Feedback

IMAGINE YOU GO TO A RESTAURANT WITH ONLY FIFTY DOLLARS IN your pocket. No matter what happens, you can't spend any more than that amount.

You sit down, and your server hands you a menu. Wow, everything sounds so good, and boy, are you hungry! But there's just one problem: the menu has no prices. How in the world are you going to stay on budget?

You awkwardly point to dish after dish with your server, asking what each item costs. It's not ideal, but eventually, you pick an appetizer, main course, and desert. You factor in tax and a 20 percent tip, and, based on your calculations, your meal comes to fifty dollars exactly. "Yay!" you think to yourself as you do a little celebratory dance in your seat.

You thoroughly enjoy the meal and feel quite proud about staying within budget. Until, that is, you receive the bill and notice a 15 percent hotel fee tacked on! *Really?!* After an awkward exchange with the server and a rather rude and unforgiving restaurant manager, you're forced to reduce the server's tip to a mere 5 percent, well below what's customary.

Then comes the last straw. As you walk out of the restaurant, you hear another waiter say to their table, "Oh, this is your first time here? I have good news—we waive the 15 percent hotel fee for all new customers." *What?! Are you kidding me?* you think to yourself. *Why didn't they offer that discount to* me?

Talk about a lousy experience. This restaurant is about to get a very sternly worded Yelp review from you later on tonight. "Two stars. Watch out for the hidden hotel fee and rude manager...Too bad, food was yummy!"

If this sounds like the restaurant visit from hell, it should. But here's the thing: this kind of experience is actually pretty common when it comes to buying B2B products, services, and software. Buyers aren't clear on pricing, what's included and what isn't, what's standalone and what's only part of a bundle, or what kinds of discounts are being offered to others.

The experience is enough to drive some buyers mad. And yet, without learning about buyers' pricing and packaging experiences through a win-loss program, many sellers are absolutely blind to everything they're doing wrong. Here's how to get the most out of this portion of your win-loss interview.

LEARNING OBJECTIVES

Unless the offering is a commodity, pricing alone typically isn't the reason an organization loses a deal. In the area of pricing, we must consider the pricing model and the salesperson's ability to clearly, concisely, and confidently articulate the model and the associated value of the model. For this reason, understanding how buyers respond to the pricing portion of their evaluation is especially important to product marketers, your leadership team, and your sales team—who is the frontline when it comes to pricing discussions.

Whether you're selling a $2,000 or a $20 million software license, buyers want to purchase a solution from a seller who can explain that pricing model and what's gone into it. Often, as we saw in the restaurant example, this doesn't happen.

When it comes to pricing, your goal isn't always to learn whether a customer thought your solution was priced fairly (though that's valuable information too). It's to learn about the *experience they had when they arrived at the pricing and packaging stage of their evaluation*. Does the pricing and packaging model make sense? Did the price equal or exceed the perceived value the buyer would receive?

One of the key priorities of pricing and packaging discussions is to determine your buyer's preferences while also getting a sense of how they feel about your model as compared to your competitors' models. As an example, if you only offer bundled packages but your buyers want a more à la carte option, that's important to know. If your approach to packaging isn't in alignment, you'll either have to educate the market on why your model is best or reevaluate your monetization strategy.

PRO TIP

Are you packaging your solution for the audience you want to attract?

It may not seem immediately obvious, but packaging is inherently tied to your ideal customer profile. This is why it's so important to gather as much pricing and packaging feedback as possible during your win-loss interviews. If interviewees are constantly complaining about your pricing but the data shows most of them aren't your ideal buyer, maybe pricing isn't your issue.

What you choose to do with that information depends on the rest of the story. Maybe you'll need to adjust your packaging to something more palatable for your ideal customer. Maybe you'll have to hire a pricing consultant to optimize your approach to pricing and packaging. Whatever the case, now that you have the data, you're able to take some sort of action that should lead to a positive result.

THE INTERVIEW GUIDE

When conducting win-loss interviews, it's important to separate "price and pricing" model questions from "pricing experience" questions. Price and pricing model questions, such as the following, will yield great insight into whether you're well-aligned with your ideal customer profile. The answers to these questions may be used to reassess your pricing model.

- How well did our pricing align with your budget?
- How would you describe our price as compared to perceived value?
- How did our pricing compare with other vendors you evaluated?

Pricing experience questions, on the other hand, will shed light on the feeling the buyer had when they discussed pricing with your sales team. Answers to these questions help determine whether pricing-related sales-enablement activities need to take place.

- How would you describe the salesperson's ability to articulate our pricing model?
- What could the salesperson have done better or differently during the pricing process?
- If the price did not align with your budget, was the salesperson willing to find creative solutions tailored to your needs? Please describe.

While salespeople regularly point to "price" as the primary reason for losing deals, it's not often the case—or if it is, there's usually more to the story. That's why it's important you use the time allocated to each interview to explore the primary loss reasons beyond price.

If your sales team records its calls, ask to listen to a few pricing discussions. Listen to how the salesperson delivers the price, explains your model, answers questions, and handles any objections.

Also, pay attention to the buyer's sentiment by listening closely to their tone of voice and noticing any subtle clues in their demeanor. Do they sound positive or excited, or do they sound confused or concerned?

THE ONLINE SURVEY

It can be useful to have online survey questions that ask your buyers to rank a number of areas related to pricing and packaging from "very poor" to "very strong," or from 1 to 5. Here are some questions you can ask:

- Please rank our price as compared with perceived value.
- Please rank us on perceived ROI.
- Please rank us on ease of understanding our pricing model.

Price Feedback	VERY Weak ▼				VERY Strong ▼
	1	2	3	4	5
Price as compared with perceived value	○	○	○	○	○
Perceived ROI	○	○	○	○	○
Ease of understanding pricing model	○	○	○	○	○

Figure 10.1

These scored responses will offer a strong dataset that can be used as a barometer to ensure your model is in tune with the market.

IS THERE REALLY A PROBLEM HERE?

You're not going to solve every pricing and packaging problem through a win-loss program, but you can expect to get directional feedback. Through this data, you should be able to determine where you're doing well and where you may want to focus more energy.

But don't leap to any conclusions yet based on a handful of interviews and survey responses. Remember, you're still in the data-collecting stage, and win-loss data is directional. The next step would be to go much deeper through a proper monetization project to really unpack whether you truly have an issue worth solving.

ACTIONS AND TAKEAWAYS

1. Pricing and packaging is a major determining factor in a buyer's ultimate decision, especially if they feel they're being nickel-and-dimed or ambushed by surprise fees.

2. As such, your goal with your pricing and packaging questions isn't just to understand whether a buyer thought your price was fair, but whether they had a positive experience when presented with the price.

3. Here, the term "perceived value" is crucial. It's not always about the bottom-line number but how a buyer understood what they'd be getting in relation to that number.

4. Think of three open-ended questions related to your business that will help you understand your target buyer's pricing and packaging feedback, and write them below.

CHAPTER 11

The Research Stage

IT WASN'T THAT LONG AGO THAT A BUYER WANTING INFORMATION on a vendor had to find the vendor's phone number in the yellow pages or dial 411, call them, speak to a salesperson, and wait for an information pack to arrive in the mail a week or so later! I remember stuffing many such packs in the early days of my career. I can still taste the glue from the envelopes.

Today, in a matter of minutes, buyers can access endless amounts of information through vendor websites, vendor-review sites, analyst reports, and online peer groups.

As I was writing this book, my company conducted an interview for our very own win-loss program. The interview was with a client we had recently won. When we asked the buyer how they heard of us, they said:

> I'm part of this really small CMO group—there are ten of us from some of Boston's top technology companies. We're constantly in touch via a group Slack chat. We also get together on a quarterly basis for dinner to share stories about what's working well and what's not working so well. Often, the conversation includes questions on various technology

and service providers: which relationships are adding value and which vendors to avoid. I leaned on this network quite heavily when I was going through our win-loss vendor evaluation. There were a number of CMOs in the group that spoke quite highly of Klue and the value they have received. This ultimately led us to prioritize Klue over other win-loss providers.

His response floored me. You're telling me there is a private, personal network of influencers from Boston's top tech companies that get together regularly to dish...and they love my company? Amazing!

The more we heard about this private group, the more our heads were swimming in the possibilities. How can we get an invite to one of their quarterly dinners? Can we sponsor one of these groups? What other under-the-radar groups exist, and do they each have a secret handshake?

No matter your industry, there are likely scores of these influential yet invisible networks. And, as it turns out, these groups are likely talking about vendors just like you on a regular basis, making them a critical resource for their members. The quicker you can identify these groups through win-loss interviews, the better! In this chapter, you'll learn how to unearth these hidden gems during your win-loss interviews.

LEARNING OBJECTIVES

If you ran a restaurant and saw that people were leaving tons of bad reviews about you online, you'd probably want to do something about it. Maybe you'd reach out to the reviewers and offer them a meal on the house—on the condition that if they *do* have a positive experience the second time around, they amend their reviews.

As a B2B company, your goal is the same as that restaurant's. A strong reputation matters. You want potential customers to be drawn *to* you, not away from you, so it's critical you understand what's being said about you and by whom.

How critical? According to extensive research on the topic, 57 to 70 percent of a buyer's decision has been made before they even engage with the vendor.[5] One study even puts the number at 77 percent.[6] For argument's sake, let's be conservative and call it 50 percent. Think about that—before you even know who this buyer is, they've already committed hours to researching you and your competitors through peer-review sites, analyst reports, exclusive invisible peer groups, you name it.

Your learning objective is to discover what those resources and channels are. Where are your buyers going for information? What resources are they tapping into—and at what stage of the buying cycle?

Your marketers and sales team would kill for this information, especially if it reveals an undiscovered influencer or helps prioritize the impact of a known resource, such as an analyst firm your company has invested in over the years.

If you unearth an exclusive CMO group, like we did, maybe you learn that they like to get together at a particular conference each year. You may decide to invest much more of your marketing budget in that event as a result. You might also make sure your CEO has a speaking spot and you sponsor cocktail hour on the first night.

Alternatively, maybe you find out events don't matter much to your buyers. Maybe instead, they use an analyst report, such as Gartner's Magic Quadrant or the Forrester Wave, to short-list vendors. And... maybe the report doesn't show your company in the best light. If so, don't panic. With this knowledge, you're able to act quickly by taking control of the narrative.

First, you can get the report in front of your sales team so they can be prepared to address any issues that come up as a result of it. Second,

5   WBR Insights, "Here's How the Relationship Between B2B Buying, Content, and Sales Reps Has Changed," Worldwide Business Research, accessed September 20, 2014, https://www.wbresearch.com/relationship-between-b2b-buying-content-sales-changed-insights.

6   Glen Springer, "What Is Modern Sales Marketing?" Gabriel Sales, November 10, 2017, https://gabrielsales.com/category/sales-and-marketing-educational/.

your analyst-relations lead will want to reach out to Gartner and Forrester to begin the process of discussing and addressing their concerns.

Bottom line: your buyers are the perfect source of intel on where people are going for information and what's being said about your company. The more you can get them to share about who or what influenced their decision, the better!

THE INTERVIEW GUIDE

There are two distinct groups you'll want to learn about during your win-loss interviews: external resources and internal influencers.

EXTERNAL RESOURCES

Remember that story back in Chapter 1 about the decision-maker on a big deal whose husband happened to have worked with a potential vendor and recommended them? That one conversation in bed determined the whole outcome of the deal.

This is an example of a resource a decision-maker leveraged to make a final decision. In this case, it was a personal network resource—a very personal network resource.

To find out about the resources your buyers consulted, ask:

- What resources did you leverage during your evaluation?
- At which stage did you leverage each resource?
- Which resource had the greatest impact on your ultimate decision?

INTERNAL INFLUENCERS

Internal influencers are internal stakeholders whose opinions or positions can directly impact the deal. Usually, these are people you work with who have previous experience with vendors in the space, control the purse strings of the deal, or have ultimate decision-making power over the deal.

Here's what you'll want to know:

- Which internal stakeholders have previous experience with the vendors you evaluated?
- What was their experience with each vendor?
- What influence do those stakeholders have on vendor selection?

The more you understand about who has the ability to sway your deal, the better.

THE ONLINE SURVEY

When writing your online survey questions in this area, prioritize learning about the external resources leveraged over understanding internal influencers. You can dig into the internal influencers during the interview.

The external resources area of the online survey is interesting because not only do you get to learn where your buyers go for information and advice during the buying process, you also discover how impactful each of those resources was to the buyer's ultimate decision-making process.

To generate that information from your online survey, ask: "Did you leverage any of the following resources? And if you did, at what stage in your evaluation process did you leverage the resource?" Then, list out a range of different resources with toggles for "Did not leverage," "Prior to engaging with vendors," "During vendor evaluation," and "During final vendor selection" next to each one (see Figure 11.1).

At which stage did the following resources have the greatest impact on your evaluation?

	Did not leverage	Prior to engaging with vendors	During vendor evaluation	During final vendor selection
Research Firm Such as Gartner, Forrester	◯	◯	◯	◯
Client Reference Call	◯	◯	◯	◯
Your Personal Network	◯	◯	◯	◯
Webinar or Podcast	◯	◯	◯	◯
Blog & Newsletter Content Such as articles, case studies	◯	◯	◯	◯
Trade Shows Such as Gartner Summit, MIT	◯	◯	◯	◯

Figure 11.1

Follow up this question with an impact question: "Please share the impact of each resource on your evaluation process." Then, list the resources again with toggles ranging from "No impact" to "Significant impact."

Which of the following resources had the greatest impact on your evaluation?

A ◯ Research Firm
B ◯ Client Reference Call
C ◯ Your Personal Network
D ◯ Webinar or Podcast
E ◯ Blog & Newsletter Content
F ◯ Trade Show
G ◯ Other

Figure 11.2

With this information, you'll get a clear idea not only of what resources your buyer consulted, but when they consulted them during the buying process and how impactful each resource was. Knowing how a buyer leveraged resources can feed into follow-up questions during the full win-loss interview.

With all that online survey data, you can now start to understand and aggregate what resources or watering holes carry the most weight with your buyers. Once you're aware of those resources, you can begin planning how to invest in and align your organization with them.

A WINDOW INTO THE BUYER'S JOURNEY

It's always interesting to see what information influenced your buyer during the evaluation process—and at which moments. Often, it goes something like this:

- They leveraged Google and consulted several research reports early on because they wanted to see which horses to include in their race.
- Then, once the race was on, they tapped into other, more nuanced resources—such as internal resources with experience in the space, their peer network, and the vendors themselves.
- Finally, once they were down to finalists, they dove into client reference calls.

That's not always the case though—which is why this portion of the interview can be so useful. For instance, you may find your buyer skipped leveraging traditional research firms like Gartner or Forrester. Instead, they leveraged an independent consulting firm with experience in the space to lead their evaluation.

Whatever the case, it doesn't take much to get to an answer. With just a couple simple questions, you can learn a lot about the different resources and influencers that contributed to your buyer's final decision.

Want to create a fantastic resource for your potential buyers? Set up a client reference call program.

When executed correctly, a well-placed client reference call can work wonders during a buyer's evaluation process. The challenge, though, is that many organizations don't set them up properly. A happy client raving about your company and your solution can be a difference-maker for your buyer. A pissed-off client can too. And if that happens, bye-bye, deal.

I've interviewed buyers who have told me exactly that. They were late into the evaluation process, down to just two vendors. Both provided references, but where one vendor's references were sparkling, the others were not so pleased. Spoiler alert: the second vendor lost the deal.

Now, I know what you're thinking: "Who would possibly screw themselves like that by putting a potential buyer on the phone with a pissed-off client?"

A lot of people. Including yours truly! Just because Joe was high on your company six months ago doesn't mean he's high on it now. A lot can happen in six months to change a client's perspective. If you're not tracking satisfaction regularly, you run the risk of having an even bigger problem on your hands—and no one wants to lose a five-, six-, or seven-figure deal due to a bad reference call.

To make sure you don't sabotage your own deals, do what one of my clients did: assign someone internally to be the client-reference program lead. It's that person's job to be the intermediary between the prospect and the reference client. A key part of their responsibility is to understand the prospect's client reference preferences and find the best match. In addition, prior to any introductions being made, the program lead contacts the reference client to ensure they're still referenceable. If they find the client is happy and everything is going smoothly, they make the introduction.

ACTIONS & TAKEAWAYS

1. Buyers conduct the majority of their research before ever speaking to a vendor representative. By the time they speak to a seller, they often already know quite a bit about your product or service and are ready to assess the finer points of your offering.

2. Outside of their own marketing efforts, businesses don't always know how a potential buyer discovered their company, what they learned about it, and who they learned from.

3. Design your interview questions so you can learn about both external and internal resources and influencers. If the buyer was referred by someone else, find out who—and whether they're part of a larger network.

4. Think of three open-ended questions related to your business that will help you understand your target buyer's research journey, and write them below.

CHAPTER 12

Sales Experience

IMAGINE YOU'RE A MICHELIN STAR CHEF AT A TOP RESTAURANT. You're hard at work one night when *The New York Times* food editor strolls into your restaurant, sits down, and orders a selection of your best dishes.

As you sweat in the kitchen over every detail, you're reassured by your lead server, who says that the editor is thoroughly enjoying each and every bite! *Phew*, you think to yourself as you high five your sous-chef.

A few weeks later, you nervously flip through the *Times* and arrive at the Food section. Your eyes are immediately drawn to the headline at the bottom of the page: "Swing and a Miss: Why Manhattan's Newest Michelin Star Resultant Fails to Impress."

That is the last time you trust the lead server's opinion!

Like the *Times* article, win-loss interviews capture many critical details that would otherwise be lost and present a great opportunity to objectively assess the buyer's view on the sales experience. What *actually* happened? In this chapter, I'll show you what you can learn once you know what's *really* going on.

LEARNING OBJECTIVES

The primary learning objective of the sales-experience section is to better understand how your sales team is performing in the field so you can identify enablement opportunities. You can bet that anything that might lead to an increase or decrease in closed deals, sales leadership wants to know about it. Let's review the primary beneficiaries of insight gained through the sales-experience portion of the win-loss interview.

THE CEO

The CEO of your average company does not have the opportunity to participate in many sales calls. Often, they're left hungry for details associated with a win or loss outcome. A win-loss report—especially one with robust data on the sales experience—gives them visibility into a process that they otherwise wouldn't have. These insights are crucial to the CEO for two reasons:

1. **Support.** By having a clearer understanding of what's happening in a typical sales call, the CEO can use what they've learned to support decision-making, such as deciding which investment may be required to help the company grow.

2. **Reporting.** Everyone always worries about reporting to the CEO. But remember, the CEO has someone to report to too: the board. And whenever an organization isn't hitting its numbers, the board is going to want to know about it. With more robust data on the sales experience, the CEO can report with confidence on what's happening in conversations with buyers, what's going well, and ultimately what actions are being taken to improve.

Remember, an informed CEO is a happier CEO. In a healthy organization, greater visibility doesn't lead to punishment or retribution; it leads to support. As a matter of fact, many CEOs come from a background in sales. When they're able to gain a view into the inner workings of the buying-and-selling process, they're in a great position to provide some invaluable guidance.

MARKETING

The marketing team is often in charge of lead generation and creating greater awareness of your company and its offerings. Product marketing in particular gets involved in GTM messaging that spills into sales-enablement activities. With better insight into the sales experience, marketing and product marketing start to get a better sense of what their sales team needs to be more effective. They seek to answer questions such as:

- Where is the sales team excelling, and where are they falling short?
- Is the sales team able to differentiate our product/service from our key competitors?
- How able are our salespeople to answer some of the buyers' core questions and address common objections?
- How effectively can sales articulate our value proposition and pricing model?
- What can marketing do to better enable sales to close more business?

Again, the goal here is support. A good marketing team has a clear idea of their GTM message and competitive positioning. They work hard to train sales on the right talk track. However, they don't always get to see how that message is ultimately delivered and how buyers respond. With greater insight, they can gauge the impact of their own messaging and determine what fine-tuning is required to yield the greatest results.

THE SALES TEAM

Sales leadership is always trying to figure out how to close more business and improve their win rates. However, much like the CEO, sales leadership often depends on the salespeople to provide updates since they don't always have great visibility into deals.

Win-loss data provides sales leaders a clear set of signposts, set by buyers themselves, that direct the leaders where to look. With more robust buyer-generated win-loss data on the sales experience, leadership can gain an understanding of how their teams are over- and under-performing. They can also get a sense of their competitors' sales motions, positioning, and general approaches.

This empowers sales leadership to focus on investments to improve outcomes in a very targeted way. In training their sales team, most sales leaders tend to focus on the basics—qualifying, positioning, understanding the product, communication and presentation skills, and professionalism. Win-loss interviews are a great way to measure how that instruction is translating into the right actions in the field.

With qualitative data on the sales experience, sales leaders gain valuable insights into how to prioritize their training efforts. For instance, they might learn their team has really strong presentation skills. Great! No need to waste any time or money building skills there.

However, that same data might also show their team struggles to disqualify leads that just aren't a great fit. Many of the deals coming through the pipeline weren't aligned with their ideal customer profile—which means all that time and money spent pursuing those deals ended up being a big waste. So, what do they do with that information? Double down on training their sales team to quickly identify which opportunities are worth pursuing and which are not!

THE INTERVIEW GUIDE

During the interview, you want your buyer to share their thoughts on how they felt during the sales experience. Some questions to ask may include:

- How would you describe your sales experience?
- How did our sales team compare with those of the other companies you evaluated?
- If you could offer one piece of advice to the salesperson in an effort to help them improve, what would that piece of advice be?
- What could they have done differently that would have changed the outcome of the deal?

Notice that all these questions are fairly open-ended. You're not guiding them to a specific answer. You're giving them a chance to speak openly about their experience. For this portion of the interview, you'll find that gathering useful insights won't be too difficult; buyers are typically ready and willing to share their thoughts about the sales team!

THE ONLINE SURVEY

While the interview is a chance to gain more qualitative data through open-ended questions, the online survey is a chance to gain more quantitative data through narrowly focused yes/no or ratings-based questions. Here, in other words, you want to understand how your salesperson is perceived by buyers in terms of sales traits (such as emotional intelligence, listening, and communication skills) and sales skills (such as ability to differentiate the product and industry and technical knowledge).

In an online survey, you can ask buyers to rate the salesperson in the following areas:

- Overall sales experience
- Listening skills
- Professionalism
- Responsiveness
- Presentation skills
- Communication skills
- Trustworthiness

Additionally, you can look at their knowledge areas, or things they've learned on the job:

- Knowledge of the offering
- Ability to articulate solution benefits
- Ability to differentiate
- Ability to address your concerns

Remember that sales feedback is an important part of this win-loss process. It provides sales leadership with the information needed to prioritize enablement activities with the goal of improving the effectiveness of their team, which ultimately improves their ability to close more deals.

PRO TIP

During the sales-experience portion of the interview, you're likely to hear some horror stories.

- "Rex was awful! I never want to speak to him again."
- "I called the sales manager and asked to be switched to another salesperson—I wasn't going to buy from you if I had to continue working with Patty."

It's never fun to hear negative comments about your sales team, but it's still valuable. With that being said, be careful who you share this feedback with. After all, the purpose of a win-loss interview is not to make a seller look bad to their peer group or senior management. Consider sharing the negative feedback with the seller and their manager in private, but redact that portion when sharing the interview summary more broadly. Otherwise, sellers will fear the program and be less likely to connect you with their buyers.

SALES FEEDBACK IS A LEARNING OPPORTUNITY—*NOT* A WITCH HUNT

As you can see, sales-experience feedback can be a very powerful tool—if it's used *for good, not evil!*

This is an important point. I wouldn't recommend using your win-loss program as a way to weed out your underperformers.

Remember that your stakeholders in this program include your sales team (see Chapter 3). You want them on your side, and you need their help to run a successful program. After all, why would any salesperson want to help you if they feel you're on a witch hunt? If the salespeople believe you're going to go dig up dirt on them—and therefore put their jobs at risk—you'll quickly lose their trust, and the program will fail.

Instead, approach these questions in the spirit of learning and trying to improve the overall sales experience. Make sure you're collecting data on behalf of a sales team that is very open to feedback, is eager to learn and improve, and understands this data is not going to be used against them.

I've worked with sales teams who felt threatened by this kind of feedback or, worse, simply disagreed with the feedback the buyer shared.

You don't learn anything from defensiveness. As a salesperson, it might feel good to dismiss buyer feedback by waving your hand and saying, "Oh well, that guy was a jerk," but that's not a recipe for long-term success.

Again, the point of win-loss analysis is to identify meaningful trends and improvement opportunities across several areas of the business, not just sales. When viewed from that light, even the negative feedback is an important building block on the way to getting better.

And for those team members who are still feeling defensive? Remind them that sales experience is just a small fraction of the overall win-loss program scope. All the insights generated will ultimately help the sales team become more effective, close more deals, and make more money on commissions!

ACTIONS & TAKEAWAYS

1. Your salespeople are probably great at what they do, but they're not a reliable source for determining how the buyer's sales experience went.

2. With an objective assessment of your sales experience, the sales team, marketing, and the CEO all stand to learn a great deal about sales' strengths and weaknesses.

3. With that said, treat the assessment as a sales opportunity, not a witch hunt.

4. Think of three open-ended questions related to your business that will help you understand your target buyer's sales experience, and write them below.

CHAPTER 13

Competitors

WIN-LOSS RESEARCH OFFERS YOU THE OPPORTUNITY TO NOT ONLY understand how you're perceived in the marketplace, but also how your key competitors are perceived. With some well-phrased questions, you can get a deep view into their reputations, how they're differentiating, their strengths and weaknesses, how they sell, and even how they're priced.

In that spirit, it is certainly fair game to dedicate a healthy section of your win-loss interview to your competition. What better way to get a deep and current understanding of your competitors than by hearing directly from those buyers who just recently evaluated their offerings?

When you know what your buyers like and dislike about your competitors, you can paint a clearer picture of how to best differentiate your offering and structure smart and effective GTM activities. In this chapter, I'll explore how to get the most out of this portion of your win-loss interview in order to give your sales team—and your company—a competitive edge.

LEARNING OBJECTIVES

Many stakeholder groups within your organization will benefit from a glimpse into your competition. Here's a rundown of the biggest winners from this portion of your win-loss program.

COMPETITIVE INTELLIGENCE

This one should be obvious. Naturally, the person or team responsible for competitive intelligence at your company would be thrilled to hear any credible new insights into your competitors. I find most larger companies have a dedicated competitive-intelligence team, while smaller companies make competitive intelligence a portion of an individual's responsibilities or a shared responsibility across departments.

Whatever the case, your goal is to help them monitor the marketplace and figure out what's going on with your competition. To do this, you'll want to ask your buyers questions like:

- How are we perceived relative to our competitors?
- What do our competitors offer of value that we do not?
- What strategic moves may our competitors be making that we need to be aware of, such as new partnerships, products, and GTM motions?
- What are our competitors saying about us?

Competitive intelligence also uses the data they collect for deal-support activities. They work as an on-demand resource to provide the sales team with intel it can use to differentiate and gain advantage over key competitors in head-to-head deals. Think of all the deals that could go your way if your sales team was able to gain and act on a little additional insight.

SALES

Sales is another huge beneficiary of competitive intelligence. Sure, they benefit from all information on their competitors, but they benefit more when that intel is centralized and accessible. That's where battle-card platforms, such as Klue, are really helpful. As you'll remember from Chapter 3, battle cards include all kinds of great content designed to help a seller respond to competitive situations. A typical battle card might include a series of golden nuggets like this:

> If a buyer mentions they're evaluating Competitor X, make sure to weave in our strengths against that competitor, including the power of our AI, our CRM integration capabilities, and our 24/7 customer-support team.

Battle cards help equip the sales team with essential information on where their competitors may be strong and weak, how they may be trying to differentiate, and how they're packing and pricing their offerings—and what an appropriate response is to each point.

Win-loss data can also help your sales team better understand how your competitors' sales teams are selling. If they're performing exceptionally well in certain areas, that's invaluable information for helping you understand (1) how your competitors' sellers are beating you and (2) how you can up your own sales game.

For example, if you know one of your competitors' sales team gives lights-out, personalized product demos and your team doesn't, you can begin to drill down on what your team does well and how it can improve. Does the competitor's sales team spend more time with the buyers before the demo? Do they create customized demos specific to the buyer? That kind of information is super helpful.

MARKETING

Competitive intelligence helps your marketers better position your company's strengths against your competitors' weaknesses.

For instance, you may learn your buyers are especially interested in seamless integration with their CRM—which your SaaS product offers and your competitor's product does not. The second your marketing team knows that, they're going to double down on promoting your integration capabilities because they also know CRM integration is a key selection criterion for many of your buyers. As a result, you'll end up looking great, while your competitor will not.

This is just one example, but any information your marketing team can gain from this portion of your win-loss interview will inform their GTM messaging and marketing sales approach.

PRICING

Information on your competitors also helps from a pricing perspective. Anybody within your organization responsible for pricing can use the pricing information gathered about your competitors to design a pricing model that may better appeal to your buyers. In addition, competitive pricing information helps you determine the most effective approach to generating your initial offer, tuning your discounting strategy, or supporting any price-to-value-related conversations you may have.

BOARD AND INVESTORS

Your board members and investors love knowing as much about your competitors as possible. They're always eager to understand how you are being compared with your top competitors, what you know about them, and what you are doing to beat them. There may be no better way to get both your board and your investors excited than by sharing some new juicy tidbits about your competition and how you're going to turn that information to your advantage.

Interestingly enough, in some cases, win-loss programs originate at the board level. Over the years, I have worked with many private equity and venture firms looking to help their portfolio companies get a better handle on the competition. It's their way of adding value while equipping leadership teams with information they need to determine where to go next.

THE INTERVIEW GUIDE

Most buyers are very open to answering questions about competitors. Oftentimes, they'll volunteer the information with little prompting, offering up details you might not have expected them to share so freely.

Knowing that, here's my advice to you: be brave. Make the conversation fun. Approach the questions with an almost playful spirit, as if this is the part of the interview where you and the buyer get to dish on gossip. "Okay, here's the awkward part," you might say with a grin. "You know I have to ask you about our competition. I hope you don't mind, but who else did you look at?"

For some buyers, that will be enough to get them to spill the beans. If not, some other questions you could ask include:

- Besides us, what other companies did you evaluate, and why did you include those companies?
- What did you like or dislike about each?
- What do you perceive to be the strengths and weaknesses of each?
- What led you to eliminate (competitor) from consideration?
- What led you to select (competitor)? What stood out?
- How close was it? What could have swayed you in our direction?

Again, these are just prompts. The point here is to get your buyers talking and follow the conversation wherever it might go.

THE ONLINE SURVEY

As a vendor, you might be competing against three different companies or three hundred. With so much competition, you may not have a clear idea of who else your buyers looked at during the evaluation process. Sure, you're going to be interviewing them to learn more, but why not take the opportunity within the online survey to capture some basic competitive intelligence?

- Which vendor was the incumbent, if any?
- Which vendors did you evaluate?
- Which vendors did you shortlist?
- What company did you ultimately select?

If you can go into your interview with this basic information—knowing, for instance, the exact three companies your buyer narrowed the field down to before making their decision—that frees you up to ask much more focused questions during the interview itself.

You can begin to paint a clearer picture of who your greatest competitors are and test your understanding as it evolves. Which names keep coming most often across your win-loss surveys and interviews? Which companies make the short list most often—and which companies get *selected* most often?

Once you have a clearer picture of who you are competing against, you can build out better intelligence on how your buyers perceive them. In the same way you asked your buyers to score your company on a predetermined set of attributes (see Chapter 8), ask your buyers to score your competitors on those attributes as well.

GIVE YOUR COMPANY A FIGHTING CHANCE

Competitive intelligence is one of the most valuable outputs of a win-loss program. In fact, I'd even go so far as to say it's one of the primary justifications for keeping a win-loss program rolling quarter over quarter, year over year. Just like your own organization, your competitors are constantly changing their approach to compete with you.

Your win-loss program is a great mechanism for staying on top of those changes so you can react and respond in real time—and in so doing, prevent them from pulling out ahead of you. Think of this data as your inside track, the secret difference-maker that allows you to see the punch coming, duck, and knock them out with a surprise uppercut.

ACTIONS & TAKEAWAYS

1. What's the best way to learn about your competitors' sales motion? From the people who went through it—which is why this portion is an invaluable part of any win-loss interview.

2. Many different stakeholders stand to gain from juicy intelligence on your competition—including the CEO, sales, marketing, pricing, and even the board.

3. Buyers are often happy to dish on your competition. Keep the conversation free and easy, and you should glean some useful nuggets.

4. Think of three open-ended questions related to your business that will help you understand your target buyer's experience with your competitors, and write them below.

CHAPTER 14

Buying Process

ONE OF MY CLIENTS, I'LL CALL THEM COMPANY A, IS A MARKET-ing-automation provider. They are cool, young, modern, and rising in their industry quickly. One of their primary competitors, Company B, is Company A's opposite—older, more traditional, and more established in the space.

As I interviewed a financial services company on behalf of Company A, I learned Company A and Company B were neck and neck until the final product demo. That's when things fell apart for Company A.

So, what happened? Company A committed a cardinal sin of product demos. They failed to do research on the audience. They showed up looking a little *too* hip and modern, even though their prospective customer was a stuffy, traditional financial services firm. One representative from Company A in particular was sporting a pair of ripped jeans and a hoodie, idly checking her phone and all but ignoring the demo unfolding in front of her. She wasn't a key player on the demo team, but her presence was nevertheless distracting, to say the least.

The ultimate decision-maker, a senior-level executive, was in attendance that day, and he was so turned off that he got up and left the room halfway through the demo. He felt disrespected that Company A was neither taking the meeting seriously nor showing a true desire for their business.

And there you have it. Two companies running neck and neck. But the moment the financial services company determined Company A wasn't culturally aligned with them, they lost the deal.

Now, not every buying decision comes down to a pair of ripped jeans, a hoodie, and cultural misalignment. Often, a lost deal involves a series of small missteps or misalignments throughout the buying process rather than one big, dramatic snafu. Whatever the case, you want to understand what happened that led your buyers (1) to narrow their decision down to you and a couple of other companies and (2) to make their final decision.

In this chapter, you'll learn how to evaluate the key milestones in the buying process that ultimately led to a buying decision. What was the buying process like? What was the buyer's experience talking to you and other potential vendors? Who else did they consult as they narrowed down their decision? With this information in hand, you will know what *you* can do so you're never caught with your pants down—or ripped.

LEARNING OBJECTIVES

The key learning objective during the buying-process section of your win-loss program is to gain a deeper understanding of the key stages and milestones associated with the buyer's journey. That journey and its corresponding milestones can take many forms.

One buyer's journey could begin when they recognize they have a problem to solve. Then, they might start conducting some research and looking at different ways to solve their problem. During the research phase, they may look internally to see whether they can solve the problem on their own—whether with a tool they already subscribe to, by making a process change, or by deciding to build a solution from scratch.

After evaluating the work required to solve the problem internally, the buyer might determine they don't have the internal resources or capacity. So, they decide to look externally at different third-party software or service providers. They start to do external research, reaching out to different vendors for some cursory discussions so they can shortlist a handful of providers with whom they'd like to have deeper discussions.

During that vendor evaluation, they may tap into the knowledge of research firms like Gartner or Forrester, their peer community, or other people within their organization who have experience in the space. Whoever they consult, their goal is to keep narrowing down the field of vendors by hearing the first-hand experiences of people who have worked with particular vendors or exploring how the vendors in the space stack up against one another within Gartner's Magic Quadrant or Forrester's Wave.

After doing a little bit of second-level research, they begin to invite companies on their short list into a more formal evaluation process. They might start with a deeper discussion of their needs or send a request for proposal (RFP) out to their shortlisted vendors—which no one likes to fill out but remains a common part of the sourcing process for many large buying organizations.

Then, they might set up some preliminary product demos to get a sense of how the system works. They may move into a paid proof of concept or take advantage of a limited freemium offer to help get a feel for whether or not the solution is right for them. During this time, they may even get into sandbox environments, where they can conduct deeper usability testing.

At this point, the company might engage in pricing and contract negotiations, begin examining proposals, and ultimately make a decision. Alternatively, the findings and recommendations gathered so far might be turned over to a committee responsible for making a final decision and negotiating a deal.

As you can see, there are a lot of key milestones during a typical evaluation process. To stay organized, many buyers keep a scorecard to track how well each vendor candidate stacks up in key selection criteria areas. Other buyers may take a less formal, unstructured approach. Whatever the case, as part of your win-loss program, you want to unearth this information to understand precisely how you're being evaluated, where you're winning or losing, and what you can do to tilt the odds in your favor.

Which of your internal stakeholder groups does this information ultimately benefit? Chiefly, your sales and marketing teams, who gain a deeper understanding into the key milestones of your typical buyers. With this understanding, sales and marketing can design and deliver helpful resources that align with each stage of the buying process. As an example, an ROI calculator, showing the value a buying organization will receive by investing in your solution, may help the buyer build a strong business case and secure the necessary budget to move forward.

The buying process is one of the few portions of the win-loss program that doesn't often have a dedicated section within the online survey simply because buying-process questions are covered in other sections of the survey—like the product-demo section or the client-reference-call section.

With survey questions being covered elsewhere, let's focus on a set of smart buying-process-related questions. To begin, ask:

- When did you first realize you had a problem to solve?
- How did you go about identifying which providers to evaluate?
- Once you settled on a vendor list, how did you go about short-listing them?
- What were the key proof-point moments?
- What internal or external resources did you tap into along the way?

Through these questions, you'll be able to piece together a buying journey similar to the one I shared at the beginning of this section. Much of this information won't be particularly new or surprising. After all, most selling organizations have a good sense of what the buying process is like for the people they sell to. At a macro level, you likely understand what a buyer goes through when evaluating different options. The key here is to gain an understanding of the most significant moments that influence the outcome. To do that, ask questions such as:

- Once you got down to the short list, what were the final decision criteria that made you go with one company over another?
- Tell us about that internal process. Who was involved? Was there pushback? Was there a debate? Were there key components that made you choose Company A over Company B in the eleventh hour? If so, what were those factors?

Questions like these can help get you to your ripped-jeans moment. For instance, during one win-loss interview where I asked these questions, the buyer said, "The salesperson called me on a Sunday while I was at my kid's football game to ask me if I had an update on our evaluation. That was the moment I decided I wasn't going to sign up with them. They crossed the line. It didn't help the salesperson's cause that my son's team was getting its butt kicked!"

Of course, these conversations can unearth some positives too. For instance, I once heard another buyer say, "My salesperson sent me flowers when my father passed away. That meant a lot."

Whatever the case, these responses are a chance to surface those moments that (1) set you ahead or behind your competition or (2) contributed to higher or lower vendor-evaluation scores. While the bones of most buying processes are similar, the key is to identify which moments or resources meant the most to the buyer you're interviewing. Inevitably, you'll find there are not only those things you did well and not so well, but also things your competitors did well and not so well. After all, it's often a competitor's fumble during an evaluation process that puts the puck in your goal!

BUYING PROCESS IS EVERYWHERE

During a typical win-loss interview, you're likely to learn a lot about the buying process throughout the conversation, not just during this specific portion. In some ways, you could think about the entire win-loss interview as a conversation about the buying process. During this dedicated portion, however, use the opportunity to dive deeper and uncover the key moments that swung a deal in your favor...or against it.

ACTIONS & TAKEAWAYS

1. In B2B sales, buyers often interact with a variety of people representing your organization during the evaluation and demo processes. Whether they realize it or not, each of these people has the power to make or break a deal.

2. Of course, the people in your company are just one part of the buyer's journey, which also includes research, demonstration, and contract negotiation. A win-loss interview helps you determine where your sales are being won or lost—and what you can do to fix your approach.

3. Think of three open-ended questions related to your business that will help you understand your target buyer's buying process, and write them below.

CHAPTER 15

Product Demo

REGARDLESS OF WHAT HAPPENS LEADING UP TO A PRODUCT DEMO, many deals are won or lost at this critical point in an evaluation.

Just consider your own experience for a moment. I'm sure there was a point where your organization was looking for a solution to make a part of your job a little easier. You got down to a couple vendors, and then you invited them in so you could take their respective products out for a test spin.

Company X's demo rocked on all fronts. Not only did the product actually work (which is always a plus), their presentation was impeccable. How? Company X took the time to conduct some serious pre-demo discovery. Weeks before they even walked into the room, they were asking you question after question about what you were looking to learn through the demo process, what would make the demo successful for you, who would be attending the demo, and what was each participant's interest in the solution.

Come demo day, this care and forethought is on full display. First off, the presentation itself is stellar. The demo is carefully designed to mirror your business. They've even rebranded it—using your company's logo and color scheme, populating the demo instance with your own content, and tying it all together with a use case that matches your own. They're confident, they answer all your questions, and in almost every way, they help you see how you and your organization could benefit from this solution. It's akin to taking the latest Porsche out for a test drive—top down, wind blowing through your hair, and a grin from ear to ear.

Company Y's demo, on the other hand, does not rock. At best, it's like a third-grade band performance—a bit off-key and not over soon enough. Instead of tailoring the demo to your use case, they offer up a generic imaginary scenario. "Imagine your company is located in Neverland," the rep says, droning through the same routine he's given to five other people that day. "I'm going to walk you through all the different scenarios Peter Pan might encounter."

Now, unless you're Peter Pan or Captain Hook, it's unlikely you're going to be very compelled by Company Y's presentation. It doesn't matter if their solution is better. If they're not going to take the time to learn about your business and your particular use case and show you how their solution solves your specific problems, why should you give them the benefit of the doubt?

This may sound a little like a fairytale, but believe me, it's not. There are far more Company Ys out there than you might think—and I would know. After all, I've conducted win-loss interviews on behalf of many of them. Buyers often point to the product demo as a crucial turning point in the buying process—especially if things didn't go particularly well for one vendor or another. It's never a good feeling to hear how you botched the demo, but at least these companies got a chance to learn an important lesson and take the right actions to remedy the situation.

When you're a buyer, it's easy to spot the differences between a good demonstration and a bad one. When you're the vendor, however, you may not be as aware of your own shortcomings or bright spots as you have no basis for comparison. In this chapter, you'll learn how to get the inside scoop on how your product demos stack up so you can make sure your company ends up on top.

LEARNING OBJECTIVES

For this part of the win-loss interview, there are two main stakeholder groups who are especially interested in learning how your product demo went:

- **Sales engineers.** In most organizations, especially those that sell highly technical products, this is the group that actually delivers the product demos. (They may also be responsible for other tasks as well, such as client onboarding, integration, and different product-related work streams.) During the demo, sales engineers team up with the salesperson to cover both the business and technical sides of the solution. They are considered subject matter experts (SMEs) on all things related to their product. Ideally, they are equipped to go toe to toe with both a technical buyer and a non-technical buyer.
- **The sales and sales-enablement team.** A lot of the success of a demo falls to the sales team, who need to make sure that going into the demo, they have a solid understanding of who's going to be in the room and what each person is looking for during the demo. Is it going to be the C-suite and business users, or is it going to be the more technical folks who are interested in hearing about data privacy, integrations, and architecture? By understanding what each participant hopes to get out of the demo, they improve their odds of the demo being a hit.

While these stakeholders approach the demo from different angles, ultimately, both groups are interested in the same thing: insights that enable them to fine-tune their approach toward setting up, designing, and delivering successful product demos that lead to more wins!

THE INTERVIEW GUIDE

The demo-experience portion of a win-loss interview often yields insights that lead organizations to bolster their internal demo-enablement process, hire additional people focused on customizing demos for strategic opportunities, or even subscribe to one of the latest and greatest demo-delivery tools. To understand where to invest, it's important to flesh out how your audience felt about their product-demo experience by asking a variety of open-ended questions:

- Please describe your overall demo experience.
- Ultimately, did the demo help or hurt us?
- How well did the demo align with your expectations and the expectations of others who participated?
- What do you think the demo team did well?
- What advice would you give to the demonstrator in regard to things they could have done better?
- How did our demo compare with those of other providers?

THE ONLINE SURVEY

Unlike in the live interview, where open-ended questions work well, use the online survey to ask specific questions about the demo experience. Not only will this help you build more robust data, it will help you focus your questions ahead of any potential interview.

Here is what a sample questionnaire would look like:

1. Did you participate in a product demo? (Yes or no.)

2. Rate your demonstrator in the following areas on a scale of 1 to 5:
   A. Overall demo experience
   B. Alignment with your use case
   C. Alignment with your audience
   D. Clarity
   E. Demonstrator preparedness
   F. Ability to answer your questions

3. Which best describes your feeling about the vendor following the demo?
   A. We felt quite confident that this solution could address our needs
   B. We were unsure whether this solution could address our needs
   C. We felt the solution could not address our needs

4. Did the demonstration help or hurt your business case in selecting the vendor?
   A. Helped the business case
   B. Was neutral
   C. Hurt the business case

Please rate your product demonstration experience in the following areas

	1	2	3	4	5
Overall demo experience	☆	☆	☆	☆	☆
Alignment with your use case	☆	☆	☆	☆	☆
Alignment with your audience	☆	☆	☆	☆	☆
Clarity of demonstrator	☆	☆	☆	☆	☆
Preparedness of demonstrator	☆	☆	☆	☆	☆
Ability to answer your questions	☆	☆	☆	☆	☆

Figure 15.1

Which best describes your feeling about the vendor following the demo?

	1	2	3	4	5
We felt quite confident that this solution could address our needs	☆	☆	☆	☆	☆
We were unsure whether this solution could address our needs	☆	☆	☆	☆	☆
We felt that the solution could not address our needs	☆	☆	☆	☆	☆

Figure 15.2

Did the demonstration help or hurt your business case in selecting the vendor?

○ Help
○ Hurt
○ No impact

Figure 15.3

Gathering answers to these survey questions prior to the interview itself will provide you a strong idea of the buyer's demo experience and its overall impact on the deal outcome. By collecting this data across many deals, you can begin to understand whether your demo is a bright spot for buyers or more of a dark spot. You can also narrow your focus to what steps may need to be taken to ensure the demo is a home run each and every time.

MAKING THE GRADE

One year, for our anniversary, my wife and I went out to dinner at a fancy restaurant in a Cape Cod hotel with a beautiful view of the bay. After we were seated, the maître d' smiled at us and said, "We know it's your anniversary, and we really want to thank you for choosing to spend time with us on your special day."

They then proceeded to give us an anniversary card placed on a fancy serving tray. And if that wasn't enough, at the end of the meal, they gave us a special dessert to celebrate the occasion.

Turned out, my brother was in on it. He contacted the restaurant and arranged for them to send us drinks. But while his thoughtful gesture was much appreciated, the restaurant clearly did some research of their own. They knew we had come here a couple times before, and they went out of their way to make sure we came back again.

That was an A-plus experience.

Deals are won or lost on the demonstration. You can invest money, time, people, and effort getting to the point of the demonstration only to crash and burn.

No one wants that.

When you're selling something of strategic value—whether it's worth a couple thousand dollars, a couple million dollars, or a couple hundred million dollars, the process is the same. Take the time to ask the right questions beforehand, make the buyer feel like you heard them, do the research, and put your best foot forward to build a demonstration that is memorable in a good way!

Outside of having a good product (which if you don't, you've got other problems), the demo is one of the best tools you have to help sway a buyer in your direction. You always want to put in A+ effort, whether you think your chances are strong or not.

To do that, you need to understand how you're performing. How are your buyers responding to your current demo process? Did your buyers get what they were looking for out of your demonstration? If not, what would increase your chances of success?

With interview and survey data, you can leverage the demo stage to gain a significant competitive advantage. Up to that point, it's often anyone's game.

ACTIONS & TAKEAWAYS

1. Is your product demo personalized to the needs of the company you're selling to, or are you taking them on a trip to Neverland?

2. Sales are often won and lost at the demo stage. To understand why, ask lots of open-ended questions related to the entire demo experience. Typically, your buyer will have very clear feedback to share with you.

3. Think of three open-ended questions related to your business that will help you understand your target buyer's product-demo experience, and write them below.

CHAPTER 16

The Hail Mary Question

"WHAT FINAL PIECE OF ADVICE WOULD YOU PROVIDE TO OUR client, in the spirit of continuous improvement?"

I was conducting a win-loss interview that had been going nowhere. Sure, the buyer provided a few useful answers, but I was worried the conversation wouldn't lead to anything of particular value for my client. Hoping to get something good as the clock ticked down, I asked him one last open-ended question.

His answer couldn't have been more perfect.

"Oh, I've got thoughts on this one," he said as a spark lit up his eyes and he straightened in his chair. "I would tell them they need to treat their people better. As part of my process, I checked out their Glassdoor reviews and found they had a lot of unhappy employees, past and present. If they're so dysfunctional they look this bad on Glassdoor, that gives us a pretty clear view into their organization, how they operate, and how they treat their employees—and that's gonna impact our decision to either work with them or not."

The buyer leaned back in his chair. "So, I recommend they treat their people better, that they do more to focus on strong morale and just an overall better working environment."

I hadn't expected an answer like this. Neither had my client. None of the data had pointed to organizational culture as an area of buyer concern, and none of my questions directed the buyer to reflect on culture. And yet, thanks to this Hail Mary question, I now had a key insight into why my client lost the deal.

In football, a Hail Mary is a super long pass, often made in desperation by a team that is down by five or six points at the end of the game. During a Hail Mary play, the quarterback heaves the football toward the end zone, hoping one of his receivers will jump up and catch the pigskin to steal the win.

In a win-loss interview, the stakes aren't so dramatic. But just like the Hail Mary pass in football, when you ask the Hail Mary question at the end of your interview, you never know what you're going to get. It could be nothing at all, or it could be the key piece of information that brings the whole interview together.

In this case, that final gut-shot response became a key actionable insight. Sure, the last thing any business wants to hear is they have a culture problem. But if they were ever going to address that problem, first they needed to bring it to the surface.

That's what this chapter is about: giving your organization one last opportunity to learn something valuable by asking a big, open-ended question.

THE FINAL QUESTION

As you've seen throughout Part 2, most of the interview or online survey questions I recommend are very targeted: "What were your business drivers?" "Who else was involved in the evaluation?" "Who else did you look at?" Those questions are open-ended to a degree, but they're specific to a part of the buyer's journey. By contrast, the Hail Mary question isn't specific to any particular part of the journey. It's just a chance for you to scrape the bottom of the brownie pan to get that last tasty morsel.

There are plenty of different ways to phrase the Hail Mary question:

The insights from win-loss programs don't always directly apply to sales or marketing. In the previous example, where the organization had a culture problem, the sales and marketing teams likely had no idea what steps the company would (or would not) take to address that issue—but at least they now knew there *was* a problem. However, the head of human resources, not one of the obvious stakeholders, would love this feedback and would know exactly how to act on it.

- What did I not ask you that I should have?
- What else do I need to know? What did we not talk about that you think is important?
- What single piece of advice would you provide to the organization that you think would be most meaningful? Where could they improve the most?
- If you became CEO of that company tomorrow, where would you invest in the business? What changes would you make?

However you ask it, the core question is always the same: "What do you want to share that you haven't had the opportunity to discuss yet?"

It's a simple ask, but as you saw from my story, it often opens the door to some of the most valuable, unexpected responses. This is where the unplanned fringes of the discussion start to form, after you've already established the core of your interview. Other insights I've learned through Hail Mary questions include:

- **Over-aggressive salespeople.** I had one angry buyer complain his salesperson called him no fewer than five times a day during the weeks leading up to their end of quarter in a desperate plea to get them to sign a contract they weren't interested in pursuing.
- **Poor reputation.** Many buyers I've spoken to have told me about

how they were impressed by their seller in a lot of ways, but they'd heard too many negative things about the company to ultimately do business with them.

- **Gossip.** Similarly, I've had many buyers share gossip they heard on the street and how that gossip influenced their perception. One buyer once told me, "I should mention I talked to my colleague who used to work at another company, and he told me the vendor is not doing that well as a business. He heard rumors they're either going to file bankruptcy or be acquired by somebody, and that killed it for me." The rumor may or may not be true, but now your team knows what other people are saying about you.

- **Product deficiencies.** In win-loss interviews, buyers have ample opportunities to offer product feedback, but sometimes, that final open-ended question will loosen them up a little and give them the excuse they need to say what they really want to say. For instance, when I asked one buyer what she would do if she were the CEO, she said, "I would invest more in developing my mobile capabilities because you suck at that."

- **Honesty.** Sometimes, the answers are just a way to improve the accuracy of information. For instance, a buyer may have given you one answer when they were asked why they didn't go with your company, but when you ask the Hail Mary question, you'll get the *real* answer. More than once, I've heard a buyer share something like, "Hey, I should mention we're going to be acquired, and the company that's acquiring us uses your competitor, so we're going to use them too. No fault of yours. We liked you. We might've used you, but other factors forced us to go with your competitor."

See what I mean? Cast a wide net, and you'll be surprised at the depth and variety of feedback. This isn't rocket science; just give your buyers a chance to say the thing that's been on their mind the whole time, the thing they want to say but haven't been asked the right question to unlock.

MAXIMIZING VALUE FROM YOUR HAIL MARY ANSWERS

Now here's the big question: if Hail Mary questions often yield surprising answers, how do you incorporate that feedback into actionable insights for your organization?

Consider the earlier example of a buyer hearing through the rumor mill that the seller was going bankrupt. If you're the seller, you'll know pretty quickly whether that feedback is true. If it's untrue, you've learned you have a big, previously unknown misinformation problem out there. Is a competitor playing dirty by spreading a nasty rumor? This is your chance to find out what other problems are lurking right underneath the radar and work quickly to correct market misperceptions.

There's always *something* to be gained from those stray bits of information that come up as a result of your Hail Mary question. Just come to this question with open ears and an open mind, and make sure you record and classify their responses with the same rigor as you would any other question so their feedback doesn't get lost in the shuffle.

In Part 3, we'll talk about ways to do exactly that: turn your valuable win-loss data into interesting and actionable insights. But first, we've got one more type of supplemental interview that could lead to a whole different set of insights.

ACTIONS & TAKEAWAYS

1. No matter how well you design your win-loss interview and no matter how good of an interviewer you are, there's almost always something your buyer wants to tell you that you haven't asked about. The Hail Mary question gives them the chance to share anything else they might have to say.

2. The answers to this question might surprise you. Is a competitor spreading rumors that you're about to go bankrupt? Was your sales team a little too pushy? Now's your chance to find out.

3. Everyone likes to personalize or add their own bit of flair to the Hail Mary question. Take a moment to think about how you might ask this question, and write down any ideas below.

CHAPTER 17

The Sales Interview

SUPPLY AND DEMAND IS A POWERFUL THING.

If you walked into a grocery store under normal circumstances and saw that a loaf of bread was selling for a hundred dollars, you would never buy it.

However, if you had a starving child at home and that loaf of bread was the only food available, you wouldn't think twice about forking over that hundred bucks. When you have an immediate need in a life-threatening situation, money isn't an issue.

This is the business your sales team is in—not selling based on price but on creating a sense of urgency, perceived value, and return on the investment in your product or service.

If your sales team is complaining they lost a deal based on price, there's usually more to the story. Most likely, they were unable to clearly articulate your product's core value proposition to the buyer. Had they been able to do that, that buyer might not have been nearly as price sensitive.

In Part 1, we talked about why you can't always take a sales rep's explanation for why they won or lost a deal at face value because they might not know the real reason the deal turned out the way it did. This isn't necessarily the salesperson's fault, and they can't be expected to know all the intricate details that led to a win or loss.

To understand those details, it's important not only to interview your buyers but your sales reps as well. Marrying their view with that of the buyer's will provide a more well-rounded perspective. In this chapter, you'll learn how to conduct win-loss interviews with your sales team in a way that feels productive rather than punitive. After all, the better you can diagnose how well your salesperson understands each deal, the better you can help them add value—which leads to more sales and more commission dollars in their pocket.

LEARNING OBJECTIVES

First things first: if we're interviewing buyers, why is a sales interview even necessary? What more are we looking to learn?

If you're a product marketer, you know there's a lot left to learn.

Again, the big issue here is data accuracy. As I first mentioned in Chapter 1, the standard vehicle for collecting data from sales is broken. Most organizations just ask sales to select a reason code from a limited dropdown menu in their CRM system. Often, the options don't reflect the complexity or reality of the deal. Adding to the challenge, sales reps have very little incentive to consider their responses before selecting an option and getting on with their day. As a result, the win-loss data your CRM system collects is generally garbage, leaving anyone analyzing the CRM win-loss data with a distorted picture of what actually happened.

Of course, this distorted picture or limited view is why win-loss interviews are so important in the first place. Even in an ideal scenario, it's dangerous to assume your salespeople actually know why they won or lost a deal since they generally respond based on their own perspectives, which, I'm sorry to say, are not a reliable source of intelligence. Salespeople have strong intuition, but when it comes to the facts of what happened in a deal, their instincts often fail them.

So, while it isn't valuable to rely on your sales team as the sole source of win-loss data, their input is still valuable as part of a broader win-loss program focused on building a complete picture of the deals your company was involved in.

The process goes something like this:

1. Ask the buyer, "Hey, buyer, why did or didn't you select us?" (This is the essential question of any win-loss program, which we've been discussing throughout the book.)

2. Then you ask the sales rep the same question, "Hey, seller, why do you think you won or lost that deal?" (This is what we're talking about now.)

3. Compare the data to see what gap exists. (This is where the learning happens.)

Sometimes, the responses from the buyer and the salesperson will be in alignment. If so, great! That frees you up to focus your energy on taking your analysis to the next level.

More often, however, you'll uncover some big gaps between your buyer's perception and that of your sales rep. As you aggregate and analyze data over several buyer and seller interviews, certain patterns will start to emerge.

For instance, you might discover that when your sales rep is asked to complete the competitor fields within the opportunity record in your CRM, they cite completely different competitors than the ones the buyers list. The company your seller thought was a threat in a particular deal may not have been considered at all.

Just like that, you've uncovered a valuable training opportunity for your sales team. By teaching the sellers techniques to discover early on which competitors are actually being considered, you enable them to be much more effective and targeted in their messaging with their buyers.

If you don't know this gap exists, it's hard to focus your training efforts. Sales interviews help you identify these gaps, leading to an improvement in your sales team's overall performance and effectiveness.

COLLECTING SELLER FEEDBACK

The question now is, "Well then, how do I collect this intelligence from my sales reps?"

Here, your options for collecting seller data will be very similar to your approach to collecting your buyer-focused win-loss data. Depending on the size of your sales organization and your particular business model, you might decide to use an online survey, an interview, or both.

If you have a large sales organization with a high volume of transactions where you're winning and losing a lot of deals every quarter and the sales team is large and distributed (let's call you Group A), the online survey is probably a good tool to use to collect data from the sales team. If, on the other hand, you have a smaller team with fewer transactions (we'll call you Group B), interviews may be a better choice.

Even if you're more like Group A and decide to take a survey-first approach, you'll likely want to supplement those surveys with live interviews for your more strategic deals. Again, this is the same tactic you would use when collecting data from a high volume of buyers. Give everyone an online survey. Then, based on their responses, the value of the deal, and the research cohort you're currently focused on, decide which deals you'd like to dive into further in a conversation with your sales reps.

This approach allows you to collect potentially hundreds of responses from the sales team on a regular basis, although you'll likely only want to focus your interview efforts on maybe ten or twenty interviews per segment in a quarter. Your full-time job as a product marketer is not interviewing sales reps, so you have to be strategic about the time you spend collecting data from them.

In Group B, you can take a similar approach. You can still survey everybody, and you can interview folks; it's just a more manageable situation. Because you have a lower transaction volume, a smaller sample size of interviews might work just fine on a quarterly basis.

THE INTERVIEW GUIDE

Your sales reps are busy. You're busy too. Best to keep these conversations as tight as possible so they don't become a burden. To do that, focus on your most pressing questions. You can even send these questions out in advance of the call so the salesperson knows what you're looking for and can prepare accordingly.

Here are some questions to consider:

- Why do you feel like you won or lost this deal?
- If you lost, who did you lose to, and what are your assumptions as to why you lost to them?
- If you won, who did you beat, and why do you think you won the deal?
- What were the biggest challenges you faced in the sales process, and how did you overcome those challenges?
- If you could go back in time and do something differently in this opportunity, what would you change about it?
- What resources did you leverage or what resources would have been helpful if they were available to you?

Similar to the questions you ask the buyer, you can also ask for the seller's view on why the organization was looking for a solution, what their primary business drivers were, who else was involved in the evaluation process, and what their primary selection criteria were. But at the end of the day, your core goal is to get the salesperson's perspective on the outcome. What are the primary reasons they believe they won or lost this deal?

Now, the challenge with salespeople and this approach is twofold. First, they're storytellers, so they may go on and on. You want to be able to control the discussion, to keep it very focused on your core questions and what you're looking to get out of it.

Second, sometimes salespeople get defensive. Especially if it's a loss interview, there may be some emotion involved in the discussion. To manage this, you'll want to be clear that, like a census survey, you're simply looking to collect data that will ultimately lead to investments aimed at making that salesperson more successful. Once you have set that stage, you're often met with an open and willing seller.

THE ONLINE SURVEY

The online survey would be structured fairly similarly to the ones we've discussed in previous chapters, only shorter. Your sales reps should be able to complete it in about two or three minutes.

Why so short? Because, ideally, your reps will complete this survey at the close of each win or loss. The survey should be simple and straightforward and include a combination of essay-style and multiple-choice questions. For the essay-style answers, provide your sellers with clear direction on what constitutes an adequate response to avoid receiving a bunch of short, fruitless insights.

Here are some sample essay-style questions to consider:

- Why was the buyer looking for a solution?
- What were their must-haves?
- What were the primary win-loss reasons?
- Which vendors were being evaluated?
- What resources did you leverage during the sales process?
- What challenges did you encounter?
- Please share a few key lessons learned.

Remember, you want your online survey (and your sales interview) to add value and insight. If it is exactly like the reason-code dropdowns in your CRM system, you won't be any better off than you already were.

There's no need for a Hail Mary question at the end of these interviews. You can, of course, ask, "Is there anything else you'd like to share?" But because salespeople are such great storytellers, you may inadvertently send them off on another tangent, so deploy this question with care.

The key here is to think about how to get the *story* behind the data. It's easy to think of surveys as a series of radio buttons and dropdowns. Instead, think of this one as an opportunity to capture qualitative data by asking essay-style questions where the salesperson has to type a sentence or two. This will take a little more work to review, analyze, and report on. But this work is necessary if you want to collect data that is both useful and accurate.

A GUIDE TO PROBING DEEPER

As you collect your data, remember: take sales interviews with a grain of salt. Without the buyer's perspective on that deal, the insight by itself is going to be unreliable. I do not recommend using this data on a standalone basis for understanding why you're winning and losing deals or making important decisions. Instead, these interviews are an essential tool for spotting gaps, inconsistencies, and other areas where you might need to probe deeper. For instance, are there some things that sales seems to struggle with? Do the sellers need more training or resources to overcome regular deal challenges or objections?

In order to identify real opportunities for improvement, it's important to have both sides of the story. To do that, the best practice would be to conduct a seller interview for every buyer interview completed and then compare the two sets of responses.

Through this data-collection exercise, you will begin to understand how well sellers know their buyers. What key obstacles are your sales reps experiencing? What can we do as a product-marketing or sales-enablement team to make their job of selling easier?

In other words, rather than focusing on why you're winning or losing deals, you're learning how to clear hurdles for your sales team to be more effective in the field. Approach these interviews from this perspective, and you're bound to get a ton of useful information.

ACTIONS & TAKEAWAYS

1. Sales aren't always lost on price, no matter what your sales team says. Still, it's worth hearing their side of the story—what went right, what went wrong, and what they think the deciding factor was in the buyer's ultimate decision.

2. Again, if the deal was lost, you're not looking to play the blame game. Instead, you're looking for something much simpler: learning opportunities.

3. Think of three open-ended questions related to your business that will help you understand your seller's experience with your buyer, and write them below.

PART 3

Conducting Your Interviews

CHAPTER 18

Selecting and Recruiting
Ideal Interview Candidates

"HOW MANY INTERVIEWS SHOULD I CONDUCT?"

I get this question all the time and have yet to come up with a simple response. It's like asking how many days a week you should work out to win the Ironman or how many hours on the court you should expect to spend before making it to Wimbledon. It all depends!

To even begin to arrive at an answer to how many interviews you should conduct, first you must work through a series of dependencies—followed by a math problem. And even then, whatever number you come up with is merely an educated guess. You may need more. You may need less. Again, it depends!

That said, I understand why people ask this question: they want to get the most value out of their win-loss program. However, in my experience, *more* doesn't necessarily mean *better*. Setting a quantity-based target may feel like the right move, but it's better to focus on quality. After all, the last thing you want is to put in a bunch of work interviewing buyers only to determine later that the data you collected does not quite satisfy your needs.

At the end of the day, you need to feel confident that the feedback you've collected is so reliable you're willing to use it to make recommendations to leadership and put your reputation on the line. Will those recommendations make you a hero or a zero?

To get to that point, start by identifying which of your won or lost deals best align with your learning objectives and which do not. You can use some macro-level criteria, such as product or region. Next, you'll want to narrow your target list even further by adding second-level criteria, such as deal size, company size, industry, or other competitors known to be involved in the evaluation.

The goal of applying these filters is to create research cohorts that will allow you to identify your ideal interview candidates within those cohorts. By targeting specific buyers within a cohort, you create a set of data that is much more likely to yield defensible and actionable insights.

Rather than counting interviews, you should be extremely thoughtful about *whom* you interview. A tight qualification process properly aligned with your program goals is the best way to develop your win-loss story and fast-track your time to value. In this chapter, you'll learn how to stop racking up useless interviews and start selecting and recruiting your ideal interview candidates.

SELECTING QUALIFIED CANDIDATES

Here's the million-dollar question: if not all buyers are worth interviewing, how do you separate the quality candidates from the less important ones? Here's the approach I recommend.

ALIGN TARGETED BUYERS WITH LEARNING OBJECTIVES

Start with the learning objectives you designed with your stakeholder group and, where you're able, use those learning objectives to qualify some opportunities into your program and others out of your program.

As an example, say one of your primary learning objectives is to understand why you keep losing to Competitor A. Naturally, you can qualify in those opportunities where you lost to Competitor A and eliminate the others.

CREATE RESEARCH COHORTS

When thinking about cohorts, let's consider how a company like Salesforce might approach a win-loss program. At the time of this writing, Salesforce has sixteen separate products listed on their website that serve companies all over the world. While many of these products complement one another (think Sales Cloud and Marketing Cloud), most serve different buyer personas. Some even have industry-specific ideal customer profiles (such as Commerce Cloud, which sells to direct-to-consumer companies).

If Salesforce decided to go for quantity over quality, they may end up casting a wide net and scheduling a bunch of interviews; however, when all that interview information is combined into a single dataset, the analysis may not produce very reliable themes. Why? Because there's no way a Commerce Cloud evaluation led by a retailer and a Services Cloud evaluation led by a B2B tech company should be in the same dataset. They're completely different products with completely different use cases serving completely different buyers.

So, what is Salesforce to do? To get to reliability, Salesforce would have to segment the data into research cohorts.

To build those cohorts, Salesforce may first decide to filter the dataset by product then by region then by deal size and so on. The goal is to end up with a set of interviews that are similar in nature so the Salesforce team can identify patterns that lead to themes and reliable insights.

The key here is not to cast a wide net but to take a more targeted approach by identifying your cohorts up front, determining how many interviews you need within those cohorts to end up with a statistically relevant sample size, and focusing your interview recruitment efforts accordingly.

This brings us to the first lesson in selecting and recruiting interview candidates: consider grouping your candidates into research cohorts made up of deals that share at least three primary characteristics in common.

In the case of Salesforce, your cohorts might look like this:

- **Cohort 1:** Commerce Cloud deals aligned with retail in the United States.
- **Cohort 2:** Commerce Cloud deals aligned with retail in Europe.
- **Cohort 3:** Service Cloud deals aligned with field-services companies where you lost to Zendesk.

Once you've identified clear interview cohorts, *then* you can start thinking about how many interviews you should conduct. And as it turns out, there *is* an answer for that: *at least ten from each cohort aligned with deals that closed, won or lost, within the last ninety days.* This is the bare minimum number of apples-to-apples interviews you can expect to conduct to get enough useful data to begin identifying commonalities, running trend analyses, etc.

Once you've identified your research cohorts, then you can continue to pare down your target list by selecting the deals that made it to a later stage in your sales process and the deals that closed within the last few months—which I'll cover in the next two sections.

TARGET LATE-STAGE AND COMPETITIVE DEALS

You can lose a deal relatively early in the buying process (at the top of the sales funnel) or relatively late (at the bottom of the sales funnel). I recommend targeting the late-stage deals for interviews and leaving the early-stage deals for your online questionnaire.

Here's why. When you target late-stage buyers, by the time you interview them, that buyer has experienced everything your organization could throw at it from a sales perspective—sales development rep (SDR) qualification process and handoff to an account executive, discovery and needs alignment meetings, product demos, client references, pricing, negotiations, and so on. This will maximize the amount of value you can gain from each interview, as the buyer can go into detail regarding all aspects of their evaluation process.

Another reason to target late-stage deals is they are often competitive in nature. The further through the sales process a buyer got, the more they had narrowed the field down to just a select few vendors. Since one of your goals may be to gain competitive intelligence about other vendors, these late-stage deals are a potential honeypot of information. In fact, when building research cohorts, many program owners choose to target those specific competitors the company cares most about.

That said, not all late-stage deals end with a loss to a competitor. In fact, as everybody in sales knows, your number one competitor is often the "no decision" or "status quo"; while you didn't win, neither did your competitors.

No-decision interviews are not only a great opportunity to learn, they also often put you in a position to unstick a no-decision outcome, get it back on track, and add another W to the column!

PRO TIP

Creating research cohorts also comes with an added bonus: you'll impress the heck out of your stakeholders. After all, anyone can go for quantity. A more strategic practitioner, however, focuses on carefully curated datasets. They understand that the success of their win-loss program isn't measured by how many buyers they interview but by how many quality insights they gain by homing in on their ideal interview candidates.

TIME YOUR OUTREACH

When do you reach out to request a win-loss interview? It's a Goldilocks situation. If you move too soon, even though the buyer may have eliminated you, they still might be evaluating others.

If your lost prospective buyer hasn't actually signed with a competitor yet, they're unlikely to give you time or straight answers if you come knocking on their door for feedback too soon, so it's generally best not to reach out until you know they have definitely made a decision.

I say "generally best," though, because here is a big caveat to this scenario: sometimes a company, believing it has lost the deal, reaches out for an interview only to learn the customer hasn't yet made a decision. In these rare cases, asking that customer for feedback about the sales process actually revives the buyer's interest and gives the company a chance to snatch a win where they had formerly resigned themselves to a loss.

If you think this approach could work for you, go for it—just use good judgment, and be strategic about it.

On the flip side of the coin, if you err in the other direction and wait too long to reach out for a win-loss interview, you risk losing the opportunity to strike while the iron is hot. Four or six months after you lose out on a deal, you may still be stinging from the loss, but chances are the company and all relevant stakeholders have moved on to other priorities. Their evaluation may feel like ages ago, and they may barely remember why they chose not to buy from you at that point.

You don't want to interview a lost buyer who is disinterested and disengaged. At that point, they'll be willing to say just about anything to get the interview over with—or they might confuse the facts and mix you up with other companies they chose not to work with.

That's a quick way to poison your dataset. Your erstwhile buyer may say they didn't go with you because of your reputation, but fifteen minutes after they get off the phone, they may suddenly realize that, no, that was another company that lost out because of its reputation.

Unless they reach back out to correct their account (unlikely), the damage is done. You've gathered the data, and now your leadership is sweating bullets because they think you've got a reputation problem. All this hubbub from one innocent mistake.

In my experience, the just-right option to reach out for a win-loss interview is within ninety days of their decision to work with a vendor or maintain the status quo. If you stick within this window, the dust may have settled, but the buyer's memory of key facts is still fresh.

INTERVIEW RECRUITING

Now that you've developed your selection criteria, it's time to go after the actual interview candidates. Naturally, what you're after here is a high conversion rate—you want as many yeses as possible as quickly as possible.

There are three approaches you can take to your outreach strategy, each with benefits and drawbacks. Let's do a taste test.

GO DIRECT

In this approach, the person who will be conducting interviews—a product marketer, for example—reaches out directly to the candidates. Just like the method, the message is usually direct: "Thank you for considering Company X. We appreciate the time you spent with us and are happy that you found a fit. While we're sorry we weren't selected, we'd welcome the opportunity to gather some feedback on your evaluation experience..."

The direct method has a decent hit rate. Its major benefit is its simplicity. Give the interviewer a list of email addresses, and boom, away they go. A motivated interviewer can fire off a lot of emails in a short period of time.

However, there are several potential problems with this approach. Here are the big ones to look out for:

- The buyer will not know the person reaching out, making it a cold-ish outreach. There's no pre-existing relationship, no warmth or familiarity. This is a big reason for this method's middle-of-the-road hit rate.
- If you're pulling names out of your CRM system, you can definitely run into some data-accuracy issues. Even in a well-maintained CRM system, not all the data is accurate, and so you may end up reaching out to the wrong person, such as the economic buyer who has little knowledge of the evaluation.
- You may be doing sales a disservice; in this chapter, we've already pointed out cases where companies reach out thinking they've lost a deal, only to learn no decision had yet been made. Sometimes, this can work out. Other times, it can torpedo a deal that was already on shaky ground.

PRO TIP

When it comes to identifying your interview candidates, here's one common mistake I see program owners make over and over again: they identify all their interview candidates using their CRM system, even though they admit the data quality is poor.

Don't get me wrong. If you want to use data in your CRM system as a starting point to target interviews, fine. But don't simply pull a list out of your CRM and think you're ready to go. As we've discussed repeatedly throughout the book, most CRM data is not super reliable.

Instead, involve the sales team when compiling your list of candidates. They are an incredible resource in this regard. They have the deal details you may be looking for. Unfortunately, the majority of their knowledge does not make it into your CRM system. Sales will almost instinctively know which companies are the best program targets, which companies are safe to reach out to, and which contacts within those companies are the most qualified to provide feedback.

If you're using the direct approach, at the very least, you need to validate your targets with someone who knows the account (more on that in a moment). You should also match the seniority of the interviewer with that of the target. If you want to talk to a CIO about a $10 million software deal, you'd better not have an intern—or even a junior product marketer—making that call and conducting that interview.

GO THROUGH SALES

The second approach is to make use of the sales rep on the account to make the interview request. Explain to the rep you're conducting win-loss interviews and ask them which contact is most qualified to participate. Again, not only can they point you to the right contact, they can also throw up a red flag if the deal is still alive, saving you from all the potential headaches we've already discussed.

In this approach, the account rep initially reaches out to the buyer with the interview request. For instance: "Hi (buyer), I hope you're well. I was wondering if you would be open to sharing feedback on your recent evaluation experience with my colleague, [interviewer], who is our [role]. We thrive on feedback and would truly value anything you'd be willing to share."

This approach has a lot of upside. The account rep knows exactly who you want to connect with to get the information you're seeking. The target has an existing, warm relationship with the account rep, which leads to a higher acceptance rate.

It's also just wise to involve the sales team. You want them to feel like this work is being done for them and that they're an important driver of program success. By working through sales, you can actually get them to lean into your program and become an active supporter of it.

There's one thing you need to be careful of if you choose this approach, though: how much power you give the account rep to veto an opportunity. This can be tricky. While it's often to your benefit to empower your sales team, you can't give them veto power over potentially qualified candidates.

Another thing to watch out for is suspicion. Some reps will be naturally suspicious of your motives, especially after losing a deal. In fact, in some cases, reps will not want to expose themselves, as they know they screwed up in some way, shape, or form.

The only legitimate reason for an account rep to keep you away from a buyer should be the possibility that the deal is still alive. Work closely with the head of sales to set proper expectations with the sales team and leverage their influence to enforce the rules.

THE ASSISTED APPROACH

Both the direct and the sales-sourced approaches have their pros and cons. Luckily, there is a third approach that combines the best of both worlds. Let's call this the Assisted Approach. Here, you pull a list of potential targets from your CRM system and vet them with the sales team before you begin outreach. You can use the same email as in the direct approach, with the main difference being you copy the sales rep on the emails.

This approach allows you to get started quickly without annoying sales or chasing bad leads due to faulty CRM data. You tell your account reps what you're doing then ask them to verify the information. Initially, they will warn you off if a deal is still breathing. If it's not, they can tell you the best contact on the buyer team. They can even tell you details you can use to personalize your outreach and improve your hit rate—who works at home, who has young kids, who volunteers and where, etc.

Through this approach, you have a chance to make an ally of the sales team without giving them too much control. It's almost like you get to have your cake and eat it too!

Recruiting your targets for win-loss interviews takes a subtle blend of skills and best practices. Here are some tips I've developed through experience:

1. **Do your research.** Before you reach out to a target, learn as much as you can about them—it may help your chances of getting them to agree. For example, I once wanted to interview a C-suite executive with a major fitness company. Some Googling taught me this exec was very involved in a certain charitable organization. So, in my initial email, I mentioned the incentive (an honorarium, basically) that we offered all interviewees and that they might want to donate it to the charity he's involved with. And the approach worked! Of course, it may have helped that I also bumped up that incentive to make the donation more substantial.

2. **Be persistent but not annoying.** Most of the time, if someone is going to agree to an interview, they'll say yes within the first two calls or emails. But that's not always the case. Don't be afraid to try four or five times, spaced out appropriately. I've reached out to some organizations up to ten times before getting a yes. Cadence is important here too; communicate with the target once every three days or so. Be professional, and give them some breathing room.

3. **Mix it up.** I recommend blending phone calls in with your emails. This is a nice, professional touch, and it will also help if your email messages are going into a spam folder. In fact, you can call targets using unanswered emails as your rationale: "Hey, I'm following up on the message I sent. I'm not sure if it went straight to spam..."

4. **Offer incentives.** While it varies, we offer $50 for win interviews and $100 for loss interviews, typically in the form of a gift card or, as I noted above, a charitable donation. Now, many targets are senior executives, and $50 or $100 will be an insignificant amount to them personally. But when you frame it as a donation to their favorite charity, their mindset shifts completely.

5. **The personal touch.** As an alternative to gift cards, consider something more personal—send the target a small gift that can be opened accompanied by a handwritten card. This can really get someone's attention.

6. **Lean on sales.** When you're having trouble catching the attention of a target, don't be afraid to ask the account rep for additional help, especially if they introduced you initially. The rep may have additional info on the target that could help you break through—the contact's favorite college football team, for example. After that, another email nudge just might do the trick.

ROLL UP YOUR SLEEVES

By now, I hope it's clear that identifying and recruiting candidates for win-loss interviews is *work*. Expect to put in some time, experience some frustration, and learn some hard lessons. This is especially true when you're first building out your program.

For example, you may think of a CEO as the hardest interview to land, but I guarantee you this isn't always the case. A security architect or other tech pro may be an introvert who really doesn't want to do a phone interview with a stranger, and they may thus require a bigger incentive. Some people will be interested in charitable donations, while others are all about the cash.

You'll work hard at this stage to identify then nail down great candidates. But the effort will pay off. A bunch of random interviews without a thoughtful approach to segmentation won't get you far. That's why, to get the most out of your win-loss program, it's important to develop cohorts and carefully select targets.

After all this effort, congratulations—you know who you're going to interview, and you know they have valuable wisdom to impart. Next, it's time to maximize their value.

ACTIONS & TAKEAWAYS

1. Selecting qualified interview candidates isn't a quantity game. It's a quality game. Better to have five strong interview candidates than twenty mediocre ones.

2. Your candidate selection should be aligned with your learning goals. To do this, create research cohorts segmented according to region, deal type, deal size, etc.

3. Don't over rely on CRM data to create your cohorts. Remember back to the beginning of this book—this data is often unreliable.

4. To recruit interviewees, the best approach is to get a warm introduction from a familiar face in your sales team, explain what you're doing, and ask them to help.

CHAPTER 19

Getting the Most Out of Your Win-Loss Interviews

SO FAR IN THIS BOOK, WE'VE SPENT A LOT OF TIME LAYING THE groundwork for success. You've designed a win-loss program. You've fought for buy-in. You've worked hard to determine which deals and personalities to target. You've even designed an extensive online survey and interview guide.

Now it's game time! No matter how well you've prepared up to this point, the interviews themselves will be the single biggest factor in determining the success or failure of your win-loss program. To succeed, you'll need to tackle your interviews with the same rigor you've demonstrated at every other step up to this point. This is no time to take your foot off the gas. Quite the opposite—now's the time to accelerate.

Why am I stressing this point? Well, believe it or not, many companies screw up at this crucial stage. They have no systems, method, or plan for conducting their interviews—let alone for doing anything constructive with all the rich data those interviews produce. It's shocking to think, given how much effort goes into simply setting up a win-loss program, and yet many people arrive at this stage unprepared to execute, thinking they'll just casually join the video conference room with their cup of coffee in tow and everyone will be just fine.

Trust me, I've heard the playbacks. Those calls are anything but fine. Often the conversation goes something like this:

[*Interviewee picks up phone. Greetings are exchanged.*]

Sales Manager: Thanks for taking the time. I'm the regional sales manager and was told you've gone in a different direction. We were certainly surprised and disappointed when you didn't select us. We even had this deal forecasted and missed our target as a result. We thought we were by far the best fit. Is there anything we can do to change your mind? Have you already signed a contract?

Interviewee: Um...

If it seems painfully obvious this is a bad approach, well, that's because it is. And yet, it's a common start to sales-led interviews. This kind of direct, arrogant, and often desperate opening immediately puts the interviewee on the defensive. The sales manager joining the call can only mean one thing. "This isn't an authentic feedback interview at all," the interviewee thinks to themselves. "It's a win-back call...please don't!"

The result? The shocked buyer starts looking for an exit. They'll claim the decision was out of their hands. They'll say the salesperson did great but the company just went in a different direction. They'll even make up an excuse on the fly just to end the call.

A win-loss interview is not just another conversation—and it's certainly not a chance for a last-ditch-effort sales conversation. If you want to walk away with any valuable insights, you and your interviewers must go into these interviews with some core win-loss interview skills. These skills develop over time. You have to practice, prepare, and refine your approach from one interview to the next. Let's see if you can spot the difference in quality between the previous off-the-cuff win-loss interview and this thoughtful, carefully scripted conversation:

[*Interviewee picks up phone. Greetings are exchanged.*]

Interviewer: Hey, thanks for speaking with us. We know you're very busy, and we're grateful you have taken the time to share some feedback with us today.

Buyer: It's my pleasure. Thanks for reaching out!

Interviewer: First off, I want to assure you this is not a sales call. We're not trying to change your mind. We simply want to get better. Rest assured, any information you share with me will be kept confidential and shared only with a limited group at the leadership level to help support our ongoing improvement efforts.

An opening like this is specific, focused, and, above all, respectful. From there, the conversation is off to the races.

These are the kinds of interviews you and your team should be prepared to conduct. Just remember that great interviews take great effort. In this chapter, I'm going to show you how to prepare so that each interview is truly kick-ass!

SELECTING YOUR INTERVIEWER

First things first: if you're going to conduct successful interviews, you need to determine who the best person (or people) is in the organization to conduct these interviews. This could be you as the win-loss program owner or someone else within your company. Whoever you choose, make sure that person can represent the interests of each of your functional groups and is experienced and knowledgeable enough to be credible during the interview process. The more senior or experienced the interviewer, the more respected the interviewee will feel and the more open they will be to answering your questions.

Whoever you choose to be your interviewer, approach this step with care. You've worked hard to build your win-loss program. To put your best foot forward, it's important to select a representative who can effectively be the face of the program while gathering vital (and often sensitive) information. Here are some of the criteria to look for when selecting your interviewer.

IMPARTIALITY

The interviewer must be perceived by the interviewee as at least somewhat impartial. They need to show they have no vested interest in the outcome, only an interest in learning.

For this reason, product marketers tend to make great interviewers. They're often very curious, and they understand the product, value proposition, sales process, and competitive landscape without being emotionally tied to the outcome of one deal over another. They also understand the value of win-loss intelligence and will not skimp on the questions. Avoid using someone who's biased (sales) or too narrowly focused (product). Often, these people just want to represent their own particular area of interest.

APPROPRIATE SENIORITY

The interviewer should have a level of seniority that comes close to matching that of the interviewee. If you select a low-level product marketing associate to interview the CEO of a multi-billion-dollar company, you're sending the wrong message and may irritate that CEO. They could even see it as a sign of disrespect.

Admittedly, getting a senior-level executive to conduct a win-loss interview can be a big ask. Senior executives are busy people after all, and you may struggle to find someone from the C-suite who's willing or able to conduct a win-loss interview. Do the best you can. Stephanie the Product Marketing Director, for example, will always be a better pick than Jake the intern.

POISE

An interviewer needs to be calm, cool, collected, and unflappable. No good has ever come from an interviewer who became nervous or robotic with their interviewee. This is another reason not to use an inexperienced script-reader who will simply read each question out loud word for word. You need someone with business know-how who is confident and conversational. They'll use these traits to determine when to move the conversation along or when to pause and dig deeper. They must be able to read the room and adjust to what the subject is saying without losing sight of your learning objectives.

While the interviewer should ideally be confident and charismatic, their most important trait is that they're a good listener, no matter which direction the conversation goes. In a win-loss interview, the buyer often has the inevitable task of calling your baby ugly. That's not always easy to hear. A skilled interviewer, though, knows how to take this feedback, smile and nod, and then ask for the buyer's insights on the impact of their shortcomings.

TRAINING THE INTERVIEWER

Once you've identified the skilled and intelligent face of your program who exhibits all these important traits, it's time to train them and set them up for success. Both education and roleplay are key factors here. You want your interviewer to feel familiar with the ideal interview format and ready to go from the very first call.

As you work to train up your interviewer, it's useful to divide the process into three core focus areas: planning and preparation, warmup, and the heart of the interview.

PLANNING AND PREPARATION

Before interviewing anyone, make sure you and your interviewer have a plan in place for how you're going to approach these conversations and capture rich, qualitative data. (Again, the "casual cup coffee approach" is not a plan.) Luckily, you should already have a pretty firm plan in place, courtesy of the learning objectives, interview guides, and online survey questions you prepared in Part 2.

Remember, your interviewer won't be able to ask *all* of the many kinds of questions we explored during our discussion in Part 2. Feel free to prepare as many as thirty questions, but expect that you'll only get to cover between ten and fifteen.

Knowing that your team won't get to ask everything you want, make sure to prioritize your questions based on your core learning objectives. The best way to do this is to review the interviewee's pre-interview survey responses. Maybe the buyer thought your organization operated poorly in certain areas or that your competitor was especially strong in others. Maybe they found your pricing out of whack, or they thought your sales team didn't respond well to their concerns. Many of these answers will correspond directly to your learning objectives, while others will open entirely new areas of exploration.

In addition to preparing your questions, make sure you have a clear picture of who you'll be talking to. Here are some basic steps I recommend:

- **Learn as much as you can about your interviewee.** Without stalking them, of course. Check out their LinkedIn profile, which may tell you where they live, went to school, other places they've worked, and charitable or industry organizations they're part of, as well as their hobbies, interests, and accomplishments. Here, you're looking for points of connection that can help put your buyer at ease early in the interview. Not only will they be flattered that you took the time to learn a little about them, they'll also be impressed with your professionalism and preparedness. Just be careful not to dig too deep, as you don't want to freak them out!

- **Read their company website.** You want to have a strong idea of what their organization does. Check out the recent news section for a conversation icebreaker or two. Not only will this show preparedness on your part, it will also help you grasp the business drivers that influenced their decision.
- **Talk with the sales rep aligned with the opportunity.** Get their perspective on what happened. Do they have questions about the outcome? What would they like to better understand? In addition to serving as excellent interview prep for you, this will increase buy-in on the part of the rep; they'll be eager to see your report. (Don't allow the sales rep to sway you from your core learning objectives, however. This interview is not about them.)

With all your ducks in a row, your interviewer is ready to begin conducting your win-loss interviews. From the very first moment your buyer gets on the call, your interviewer should be working to make the interviewee feel comfortable, safe, appreciated, and respected. Here's how.

WARMUP

With the prep work complete and the actual meeting underway, it's time for your interviewer to establish an immediate and lasting connection with the buyer. This is where preparation pays dividends; by showing that your team has researched the buyer and their company, your interviewer will be able to demonstrate that this won't be a generic and scripted phone interview but rather a business conversation with a knowledgeable peer.

After thanking the subject for their time and expressing gratitude in general, start with an icebreaker prepared in advance, some sort of connection they can bring up. This is the time to lower walls. School ties often work well here, as do former employers or LinkedIn connections in common, as well as congratulations for notable accomplishments. People love to talk about themselves, and showing a genuine interest helps loosen them up.

From there, the transition from warmup to the heart of the interview should feel organic to the subject. Here, the interviewer's job is to determine when the subject has loosened up enough and is ready to begin answering questions. Feel free to pepper in a couple of softball questions, but be sure to use this transition time to set expectations—how long the call will be, how the information will be used, and whatever benefit they may receive by taking the call (such as a gift card or donation). When your interviewee knows what to expect, they're more likely to feel comfortable.

THE HEART OF THE INTERVIEW

As warmup gives way to the meat of the interview, keep it simple by starting at the beginning—in this case, the beginning of the buyer's journey. That means starting with the business drivers that prompted the subject's company to look for a solution, followed by the research they conducted that led them to consider your company, and finally their selection of a vendor.

The interviewer's job is to walk the subject down this path, stopping along the way to dig deeper into areas of importance. (Again, see Part 2 for what this looks like in application.)

When training interviewers, stress the importance of asking open-ended questions and being curious. After listening to an answer, an interviewer should have a sixth sense that tells them when to probe for additional information. *Is there more to the story here? Will my stakeholders be satisfied with their answer, or should I probe deeper?*

Similarly, a skilled interviewer knows it's up to them to control the flow of an interview. After all, they might not be able to change the duration of the interview—thirty minutes is thirty minutes, period— but they *can* control how much valuable information they're able to collect during that time. So, it's important to know when to politely interrupt the interviewee to keep the conversation on track by pivoting the conversation to a more fruitful area. They should also be hyper focused on interview time management and tracking their progress against all their learning objectives.

The key phrase here is "politely pivot." Interviewers should be confident enough to interrupt the interviewee's flow, without coming across as being rude, if that flow is not adding value. If you allow the interviewee to chew up too much time talking about their new puppy or going through their extensive work history, you risk running out of time and missing out on vital areas. A good rule of thumb here is to signal to the interviewee that you'd like to interject by clearing your throat or opening your mouth slightly while leaning forward as if getting ready to say something.

Another handy best practice has more to do with reigning in the interviewer's commentary. I refer to the practice as the 90/10 rule—the interviewer should speak only 10 percent of the time (asking concise questions), with the interviewee taking the other 90 percent. Without training, interviewers tend to overexplain their questions or ramble a bit, eating up valuable chunks of what is likely a thirty-minute interview. The 90/10 rule encourages interviewers to be more concise with their questions and keep the focus on the buyers—avoiding any annoying and unnecessary time creep.

Finally, as the call wraps up, be sure to thank the subject again, showing appreciation for their time and expertise, and remind them of the incentive they've earned.

LOGISTICS

Now that you understand how an interviewer should conduct a call, let's turn our attention to the question of *where* they should do it. Your interviewer, after all, doesn't just exist as a program in the cloud. They're a flesh-and-blood human being who occupies space in the real world. As such, it's important to carefully consider the setup of the space in which they'll be conducting their interviews.

- **Keep your environment in mind.** A good setup starts with a quiet spot. If the interviewer is working outside the office, it's important they ensure no screaming kids, coffeehouse chatter, or barking dogs are around to serve as distractions. In video meetings, the interviewer's background should be organized, uncluttered, and professional. Consider using a standard background.

- **Always ask for a "video on" interview.** While an interview can be conducted by telephone, it's far preferable to use Zoom, Microsoft Teams, or your video-conferencing tool of choice. This will help the interviewer better read the interviewee's body language, and it provides more content for your analysis team, who may take video clips from interviews and present them along with their findings and recommendations.

- **All interviews should be recorded and transcribed.** While it's always important to ask the interviewee for permission, recording is critical. The interviewer may choose to take a few notes, but if they're taking too many notes, it's hard for them to be fully present and actively listening—and in a video meeting, the interviewee will be able to see this. That said, I do suggest creating a printed worksheet of key learning objectives that the interviewer can refer to as needed.

- **Send the incentive immediately after the interview.** It's important to complete the interviewee's experience by sending them an email with a link to their incentive. Within the email, once again thank them for their time and ask if they would be open to reconnecting if you had a follow-up question or two.

As you can see, the more your team can standardize this process, the more effective it will be. For maximum results, I definitely recommend making a checklist of any process or action you will take on every call.

It's hard to train somebody to be naturally curious. It's more a trait than a skill. So, whether the interviewer is curious or not, we recommend they learn and practice a root-cause analysis method known as "the Five Whys."

The Five Whys technique was developed at the Toyota Motor Corp. by Sakichi Toyoda as a way for the company to improve its manufacturing methodologies. According to another Toyota employee, Taiichi Ohno, the Five Whys quickly became "the basis of Toyota's scientific approach." As the architect of Toyota's vaunted production system, he would know.

The essential idea of the Five Whys is both brilliant and straightforward: keep repeating "Why?"—just like a toddler asking why they can't have ice cream for dinner. As the name implies, the interviewer asks why up to five times in order to fully explore the relationships underlying a problem. By the time you get to the fifth why, the theory goes, you will have landed on the root answer, or root cause, of the problem.

In the context of a win-loss interview, this translates into digging as deep as necessary to uncover the root cause of the decision to work with you or a competitor.

THE HUMAN TOUCH

At the end of the day, the interview is only as good as the interviewer. Their ability to put the buyer at ease and extract information pertinent to your learning objectives will determine the success (or lack thereof) of your win-loss program. You've built a stellar process for info collection, but it's the data itself—collected by the interviewer— that matters the most.

In other words, with all the effort you've put into your win-loss program so far, there's no sense in going halfway now. To get the most out of your win-loss interviews, you need to be like Larry King, using every tool available to get people to open up and increase your odds of success. If you don't come in with that mindset, you won't get the valuable results you crave.

Now that you have your interview method down, let's assume you've gone out and conducted a series of interviews. You've heard some really juicy feedback from various buyers. You think to yourself, "Are these trends or just one-off anecdotes?" Now comes the fun part: analyzing your dataset to see what themes may emerge. Sounds easy right? Well, it may be easy when looking at online survey data, but analyzing qualitative, unstructured data is a whole different ball of wax. We'll go deep on data analysis in the next chapter.

ACTIONS & TAKEAWAYS

1. Conducting a win-loss interview takes skill and preparation. Don't waste a good opportunity to learn valuable information by rolling out of bed and winging it.

2. Most likely, as the program head, you will not be the one conducting the win-loss interviews. Look for someone in the organization who is poised, impartial, and of similar rank and status as the person they're interviewing.

3. Once you've selected your interviewer, walk them through the preparation process so they arrive at their call ready to go. Create a series of questions (not to be used as a script), create a welcoming environment, and otherwise eliminate as many variables as you can.

CHAPTER 20

Unpacking the Value of Your Win-Loss Data

A FEW YEARS BACK, I WAS SITTING WITH THE FRENCH FOUNDER of a marketplace platform provider who was smiling because he was so thrilled at the insights I'd been able to provide for him through his win-loss program. His then-small company had been making the fundraising rounds, and he'd just persuaded a major venture capital firm to invest $60 million.

This founder already knew he had a great story to tell about his business model and the fantastic market opportunity his company was sitting on. What he didn't have, though, was a centerpiece, something to create energy around his presentation and really drive the point home.

Using the data from the win-loss interviews I had conducted on his behalf, he began to paint a picture not of the organization, but of his buyers.

"That's when their eyes really lit up," the founder told me. "I showed the VCs how much we knew about our buyers, how our solution aligned with their needs, how well we understood our competition. They loved it." Two days later, the founder told me, the VC firm made the sixty-million-dollar offer.

(Side note: this company has since raised $555 million on a valuation of $3.5 billion. So, it's an understatement to say that $60 million was the start of something big.)

I can't tell you how many people come to my company looking for direction well after they have their win-loss program up and running. They have clear learning objectives, and they're conducting strong interviews, but they have no idea what to do with all the data they've collected.

I get that. It's one thing to collect the data. It's another entirely to do something useful with it. It's no surprise, then, that this is the part of the process where many win-loss programs falter. Without a clear sense of how to organize, synthesize, and present their findings, program leaders struggle to communicate the insights and value of their win-loss program to the relevant stakeholders.

As a result of this struggle, usually one of two things happens:

1. They sit on their mountain of valuable data, unable to unpack it, watching it gather dust until it's considered old data and no longer relevant.

2. They deliver a series of jumbled findings to their stakeholders with no clear story or throughline.

In either scenario, the result is the same: nobody finds the results helpful, everyone is dissatisfied, and the win-loss program eventually fizzles out.

In this chapter, you're going to learn how to make sure that never happens to you. Every aspect of a win-loss program requires a great deal of thought, hard work, and attention to detail. The sorting and analysis phase is no different—you just need a framework to follow. In the following sections, I'll walk you through the approach we use at Klue to transform our raw data into value-packed, actionable, and measurable deliverables.

GETTING STARTED

You've already set up your win-loss program, secured stakeholder buy-in, successfully recruited interviewers and interviewees, and conducted and recorded the actual interviews. Now you can move forward with an initial analysis.

To begin, you'll want to return to your initial program learning objectives. If you had six or eight such objectives, your first cut at analysis is to go through interview transcripts and simply collect and record any responses that align with those learning objectives. As an example:

- Why are we winning and losing?
- How is our sales team performing?
- How did we compare with Competitor A?

Assuming you were thoughtful about how you navigated the interviews, you'll find nearly all the answers in the transcripts. Identifying these moments is an important first step in your analysis.

While digging out these answers, look for any direct quotes that will provide clarity to your learning objectives. For example, if leadership change was a critical business driver that compelled the company to seek a new solution, imagine finding a quote like this one: "We had just hired a new Chief Revenue Officer who came from a company where he used this other solution. He just knows it really well, and he wouldn't take the job unless we agreed to use it."

In a case like this, you've got a key finding on a learning objective backed up by a direct quote. Be sure to copy and paste that quote in with the key finding. Then it's lather, rinse, repeat for each learning objective.

Once you've accomplished this, have an editorial team summarize key findings from the interview. These will become the sections of your summaries for your company's leadership team.

TEXT TAGGING

At this point, even though you've identified some of the answers to your key learning objectives, you likely still have a lot of unstructured data in front of you. To better sort and understand your interview content, I recommend conducting a thorough text analysis. A text analysis is simply the process of identifying key quotes of interest from within your interview transcripts, highlighting those quotes, and assigning each a main topic and a subtopic. As an example:

"I found their product to be so much easier to use than the other vendors we evaluated."

The main tag here would be "Product," and the sub-tag would be "Ease of Use."

By following this approach, you end up with a series of tag groups (Product) and a number of sub-tags for each tag group (Ease of Use).

Repeat this process for each interview with each buyer in your research cohort and create new tag groups and sub-tags as needed to keep the analysis closely aligned with your learning objectives. As you work through more interviews, you will likely see common patterns (trends) begin to emerge.

A note: while there are many tools that leverage AI to perform text analysis of unstructured data, such as our very own platform at Klue, manual text tagging, while quite laborious, is still widely used and considered by many as the most accurate form of analysis.

Whichever approach you take, AI-assisted or manual, the key is to transform your qualitative, unstructured interview data into something more structured, quantitative, and, above all, *searchable*. The best-case scenario is your text tags flow into a filterable dashboard that allows you to slice and dice the data, enabling you to drill down from macro-level to micro-level patterns.

Again, a good text-analysis tool will capture all of this, allowing you to build a dynamic taxonomy that can display key trends in the data. In a platform like Klue, this taxonomy also makes it easy to perform a deep dive into each of the specific categories. With just a click on a key quote, the program will link you directly to both the transcript and the video recording, allowing you to pick up on sentiment and study nonverbal cues, such as body language.

You can use these tools to create cool visualizations too. Here's an actual example from a client of mine demonstrating, in chart form, that the client may have a problem with overly aggressive salespeople:

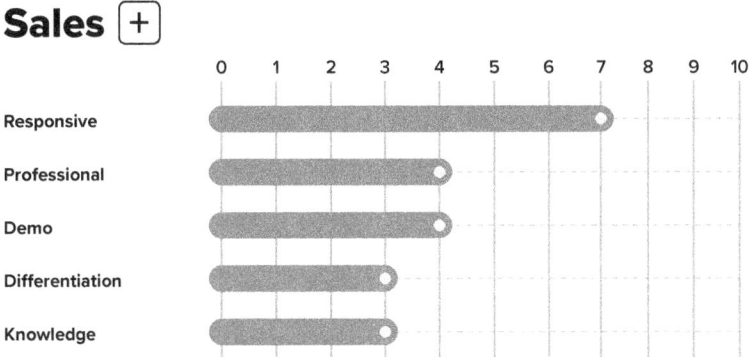

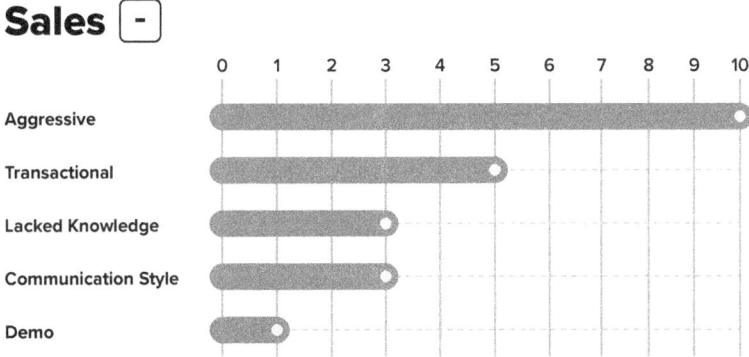

Figure 20.1: A sample graphic breakdown of tagged win-loss data indicating that the organization has a problem with pushy salespeople.

What software should you use to aggregate, analyze, tag, and synthesize all your unsorted win-loss data? I realize in today's fast-moving world, you have many options, and it's impossible to predict what options will be around three months from now—let alone three years.

When evaluating tools to sort and analyze your win-loss data, here are some questions to ask:

1. Can it both capture the data and serve as a data repository?

2. How is the user interface? It should be easy even for the non-techies to use. In my opinion, a lot of platforms in this space are overly complicated.

3. How does it stack up in terms of data analysis? Naturally, the ability to analyze content, either through AI or manually, is crucial. Look for the tool that can do the most with the least amount of effort.

4. Is it searchable? After all, what is the use of collecting and sorting all that data if you can't even find it?

These are just some of the most important considerations. Bottom line: don't go with a tool unless you're confident it can satisfy your exact business needs and won't be more of a hassle than it's worth.

TURNING INSIGHTS INTO DELIVERABLES

Once you've collected the answers to your key learning-objective questions and then tagged, organized, and synthesized all your interview data, you can now package the data in various useful ways and present it to relevant stakeholders.

There are a lot of ways to prove a point—and there are many points that can be proven. It may never have occurred to you, for instance, to use win-loss interviews to raise funds, but as you'll see in the following discussion, if you use your imagination, anything is possible.

STAKEHOLDER VALIDATION

Remember in Chapter 4, where we discussed the importance of building stakeholder buy-in and collecting input up front to ensure their interests are accounted for? Here's where that work begins to pay off. Look back to Figure 20.1 and imagine your company's chief revenue officer wanted to know more about how the sales force was performing. You now have structured, quantified data that can help answer that question—which means you've demonstrated the unique value of your program to that specific stakeholder! (Go ahead and take a moment to pat yourself on the back. I'll wait.)

UNEARTHING NEW INSIGHTS

If you've been diligent throughout the win-loss process, it's not just the CRO who will be happy. Most likely, you'll have a robust, valuable dataset for each of your key stakeholders—presentable in a way that is both meaningful and actionable. The benefits, however, don't stop there. In addition to being able to create targeted deep dives for functional leaders and other stakeholders, you can also add value by creating research briefs on emerging trends that were *not* previously on anybody's radar.

In one situation, I was working with a client who was sure their solution was far better than their main competitor's. The client was larger, well-funded, and had a strong track record of success. The competitor, however, was small, scrappy, and willing to do just about anything to win a new client. What the client found out was that the small, scrappy competitor was using their size, speed, and agility as advantages—claiming their clients had more input on product direction and should expect a much higher-touch relationship. This resulted in my client losing important deals to the competitor because my client was perceived to be rigid and slow. Whether this was true or not, it was clear the competitor's GTM strategy was working well.

New insights such as these are crucial when mounting your defense against any competitor, especially those new to the market.

DEAL REPORTS

As the name implies, these deliverables provide details on what happened in a given deal. They often include a "Key Findings" section where each learning-objective-related finding is reported, as well as important and often insightful quotes from interviews, the interview transcript, a link to the interview recording, and so on.

Each report should include sections for all the areas we covered in Part 2, including business drivers, scope and selection criteria, product feedback, pricing and packaging, influencers (research stage), sales experience, competition, buying process, and others.

Make sure to begin each new deal report with a very strong "Win or Loss Reasons" section. While many people will want to read through the entire key findings section, others will want things summarized, and a very clear "Why We Won" or "Why We Lost" section is critical.

EXECUTIVE SUMMARY PRESENTATIONS

As I'm sure you already know, executives love their summaries. In fact, if your own journey matches the story we used to open Chapter 1, an executive summary is what compelled you to develop your win-loss program in the first place.

Executive summary presentations are well-suited to quarterly business reviews, fundraising activities, and board meetings. In the latter case, mature companies will use their win-loss summaries to present reliable, honest information—even if the news is bad. A lot of good can come in such a circumstance if the board knows it's getting trustworthy data.

To create the most value for your senior leadership, your job is to identify the biggest, most urgent insights they'll want to know about and act on. Often, this will involve a presentation focusing on key findings across a series of interviews presented in aggregate. Picture twenty responses to a given learning objective or more—enough so that key themes and trends can begin to emerge.

These presentations may look like the following:

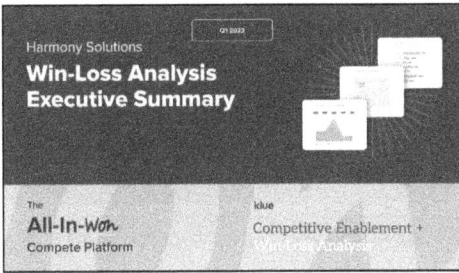

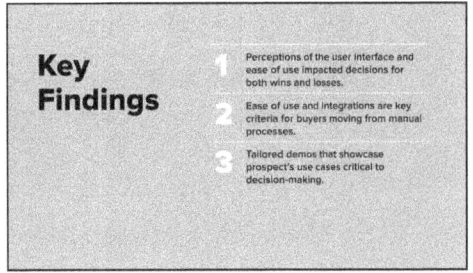

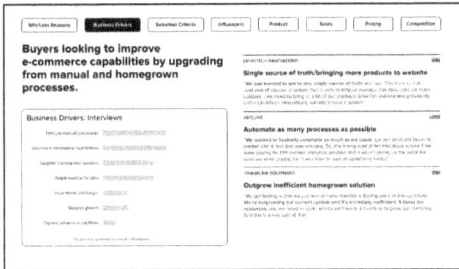

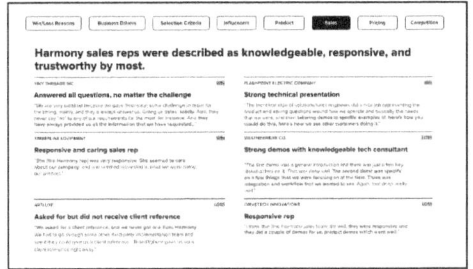

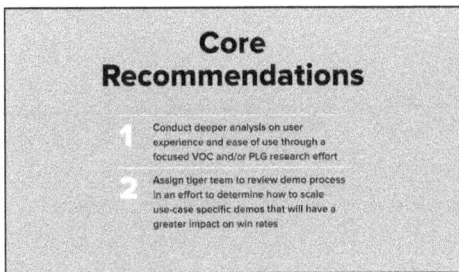

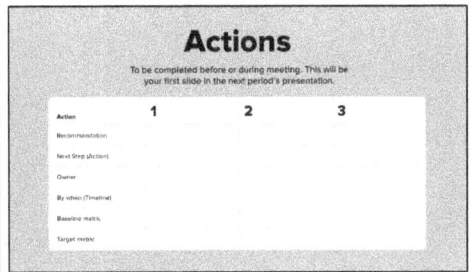

Figure 20.1

However you present your data, make sure you're focused on the biggest question any executive is going to ask: "What do we do now?" The greatest value of these presentations is that they allow your leadership team to develop a strategy and set of tactics to capitalize on your insights.

By peppering senior leadership with a regular dose of program updates—and, most importantly, actionable insights—you will be able to demonstrate the value of your win-loss program at the highest levels of the organization.

SALES TEAM PRESENTATIONS

These deliverables can be used both to recognize the good work your sales team is doing (don't forget the "win" in "win-loss interview"!) and coach salespeople so they can more consistently hit their targets. In kickoff meetings especially, these presentations are excellent tools for letting the sales team know how customers perceive them—where they do well and where they need improvement.

As we've discussed at other points in this book, when win-loss info is combined with other data, sales organizations can then create "battle cards" that provide excellent ammunition for reps, showing them how to respond when buyers raise challenging objections or when they're up against a specific competitor.

Of course, in most companies, the marketing team creates the materials used by sales to support its selling activities. We'll get to them in a moment.

PRODUCT

For product groups, win-loss reports offer invaluable intelligence on how the product is helping to win or lose deals. Data from interviews might demonstrate, for example, that you're losing deals because your company's experience with mobile is shaky or you lack integration with a key technology platform.

Having this information at your fingertips during visioning meetings can help the product team develop a roadmap to close these gaps.

PRO TIP

Always seek, and receive, permission to use a quote from a win-loss interview. Tempting though it may be, you cannot simply cut and paste a glowing review into marketing materials.

MARKETING

Marketing can use win-loss reports to feed into its asset creation and design process. The reports can help the team create relevant, responsive websites; GTM assets; and sales decks.

Additionally, key quotes from interviews serve as excellent proof points. Prospects trust the opinions of other buyers, so it can be an extremely powerful tactic to deploy a choice quote or two to demonstrate why somebody chose to work with your company.

PARTNER PRESENTATIONS

Another use case for win-loss reports, and one that's often overlooked, is in presentations to partners. If your company has partner summits, reports generated from win-loss interviews can provide a wealth of information that those partners wouldn't otherwise learn.

These deliverables can demonstrate to your partners what buyers think about your partnerships in general and their company in particular. Partners can then gain valuable insight into how they are perceived, and they'll be grateful to you for any nuggets of information you turn up.

DON'T BE AFRAID TO THINK OUTSIDE THE BOX

As you consider how to best leverage your win-loss data to add value within your organization, remember that the options explored in this chapter are just starting points. In fact, I've found that the organizations that create the most novel ways to leverage win-loss information are the ones that often benefit most from these programs—like that founder who turned a win-loss report into a $60 million investment.

To get the most out of your program, continuously ask yourself:

- Who can I serve with this information?
- Who should I meet with and walk through the data?

- How can I leverage this intelligence to drive value across the organization?
- Where should I get started?

When you keep the focus on results—on what you want to learn and how that knowledge will serve your organization—the path to getting there becomes much clearer. The key is to have a reliable model you can follow, a reliable platform to help you aggregate data and drive insights, and the willingness to do the legwork necessary to produce results.

If you can do that, then the world is your oyster. Stakeholders across your organization will be aligned with clarity and purpose. Even better, they'll see the real value a robust win-loss program can bring to the table.

From there, it's all about turning that clarity into concrete action.

ACTIONS & TAKEAWAYS

1. Now that you've collected all that win-loss data, what do you do with it? Win-loss interview data can be used in a lot of different ways. It can even help a company prepare a compelling story for their next fundraising round!

2. Once you've collected the data, the next step is to analyze it. One useful approach is a thorough text analysis: identify potentially useful or meaningful quotes and create appropriate tags to sort different parts of the interview into meaningful groups.

3. Once you've sorted your interview data, examined the trends, and deciphered a meaningful story from them, it's time to share those stories with all the different stakeholders you recruited at the outset of your program.

CHAPTER 21

How Do You Drive Action?

HERE'S A SCENARIO I'VE SEEN TOO MANY TIMES.

Somebody builds a strong win-loss program. They take owner-ship of the program, they work hard at it, and the program regularly produces useful insights.

But the program owner is a one-man band. They're good at what they do, but no one else knows exactly what their work entails. Then, when the program owner moves on to another business unit or company, poof—a once thriving program dies, just like that.

Now consider a much happier scenario: in one company I recently worked with, the person who built the program took the time to create and nurture a strong win-loss committee. He may have run the show, but others knew how he operated.

More importantly, the committee helped the program owner turn his work into results. In one instance, acting on a set of win-loss findings, the committee chair realized they had a massive unrealized sales opportunity in the healthcare sector. So, they assigned a repre-sentative from marketing to build a data sheet that would improve their sales process specific to the healthcare sector.

Six months later, the committee was able to report that healthcare wins had risen by 50 percent. And with such a massive, obvious net gain for the company, support for the win-loss program grew—with members of the C-suite throwing their weight behind it.

The lesson? Two things. One, if you want your win-loss program to last, don't be a one-person show. Two, if you want your win-loss program to *drive action* and impact your business, you're going to have to work with others to operationalize your program and its insights.

That's what this chapter is all about. Remember all the way back in Chapter 3, when we talked about the importance of creating a team of dedicated stakeholders? This is where that work pays off.

WIN-LOSS COMMITTEE, ASSEMBLE!

No matter how your insights and reports sparkle, no matter how much they could potentially help the company, they won't receive the attention they deserve without help from others.

This is, of course, easier said than done. Operationalizing a win-loss program involves change, and instituting any change in any organization is often met with resistance. You're essentially asking people to form a new committee, do more work, and put their reputations on the line in a new way.

Given this challenge, it's no wonder the operationalizing stage is where many otherwise strong programs fall apart.

This is why I encouraged you to find your stakeholders in Chapter 3. You need a team who is just as dedicated to the program's success as you are. They should have a personal interest in the outcomes. By identifying them early, you'll be much more likely to form an engaged, successful committee. Here's how to set up a win-loss committee that actually functions.

WELCOME TO THE CLUB!

This committee will review win-loss data together. Members will decide which of that data requires action, what that action should be, and who gets assigned the task. So, it's important they be people who can drive change within the business.

The exact composition of your committee will vary depending on your needs, but members should be drawn from across the organization, including those from:

- Sales and marketing leadership
- Customer success
- Product marketing
- Product management and engineering
- Competitive intelligence
- The C-suite (sponsorship at least, and ideally participation)

To a degree, the composition of this committee should reflect the learning goals you established during your initial outreach. If customer success isn't a large priority, for instance, then a stakeholder from that team might not be essential to the committee.

DESIGNATE A PROGRAM CHAIR

With your win-loss committee assembled, next you'll need a program chair. This person will herd the other members, holding them accountable for meetings and deliverables.

Naturally, to be an effective chair, this person will need to dedicate the most time to the win-loss program, which in turn means they must believe in it. This is why, typically, the chair is the person whose department owns the program and who's spearheading it—often from product marketing.

SET THE SCHEDULE

One of the chair's first tasks will be to set up regular, and fairly frequent, committee meetings. It's important these meetings are considered a high priority for all involved. If meetings are frequently rescheduled, the program will flounder as your committee members focus their energy on competing priorities.

Set Meeting Cadence

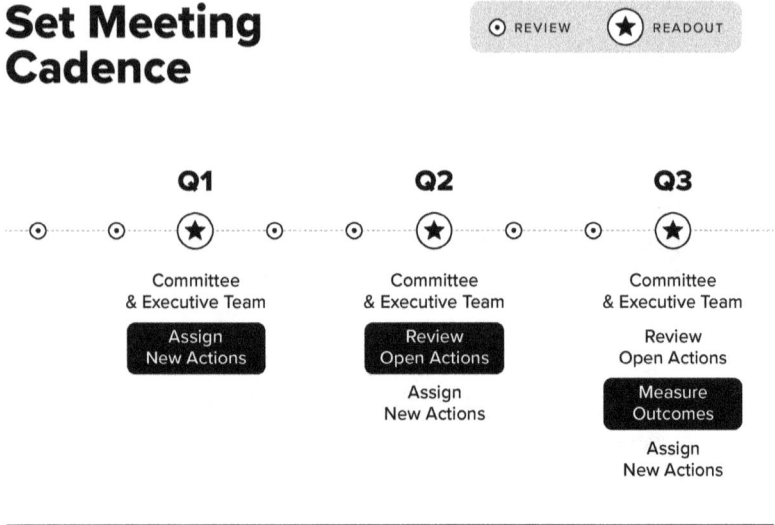

Figure 21.1 shows a suggested cadence for these meetings.

As illustrated, the meetings will have varying goals and agendas. They will begin with a set of review meetings to walk through the win-loss interview summary reports. All members are expected to read the reports (or at least key findings) before each meeting and be prepared to discuss the findings from their vantage point within the company.

Again, this is why it's vital to have representation from multiple departments. Sales, product marketing, and competitive intelligence may all have very different takes on the same dataset. By hearing everyone's perspective, the committee can set priorities and then map out a course of action.

Generally, after two review sessions—typically once a month—the next meeting involves the senior leadership team, and perhaps even the board. In this meeting, the committee presents an aggregate view of a quarter's worth of win-loss data to senior management along with recommendations for acting on that data. These recommendations must be specific and prioritized.

Once the program gets rolling, another agenda item is added to the quarterly meetings: an update on the results of actions taken at the *prior* quarter's meeting. Measuring outcomes this way proves your program is bringing positive change to the organization.

For example, let's say that through win-loss interviews, the committee learned the company was losing deals because sales reps didn't have quick access to pricing information—it takes too long to get a quote. As a result, the committee began measuring cycle times. The problem was confirmed, so the committee (with senior leadership) invested in tools to make pricing info more easily available.

By the time your program has been operating for a while (nine months at the most), you should be able to measure a reduction in sale-cycle time. That's a clear win brought about by the win-loss program. A problem was identified, changes were made, and those changes resulted in measurable benefits.

Now that you understand the general composition and meeting frequency of your win-loss committee, let's zoom in to look at how these meetings turn insight into action.

Capture Actions

INSIGHT	ACTIVITY	METRIC	MARKETING	PRODUCT	COMPETITIVE INTEL	ENABLEMENT	SALES
Buyers not convinced we understand them	Create industry-specific content	Win rate by Industry	R	I	I	C	A
Competition has come out with new GTM	Refresh compete training program	Win rate by Competitor	C	I	R	A	C
Demos are too generic	Demo process overhaul	Demo satisfaction score	A	R	I	C	C
Losing deals based on UI/UX	UX review & recommendations	UX satisfaction scores	C	R	I	I	C

R	**A**	**C**	**I**
RESPONSIBLE	ACCOUNTABLE	CONSULTED	INFORMED
The team member who does the work to complete the task.	The person who delegates work and provides final review on a task or deliverable before it is complete.	People who provide input on a deliverable based on the impact of their work or their domain of expertise.	People who need to be kept in the loop on project progress.

Figure 21.2

In order to capture actions effectively in your win-loss committee meetings, I've found the RACI framework to be most effective. First introduced in the 1950s, RACI was developed by Edmond Sheehan, who was known for his work on responsibility charting and organizational structure. RACI is an acronym for the following:

- **Responsible.** The member who does the work to complete this task.
- **Accountable.** The person who delegates work and provides final review on a task or deliverable before it's deemed complete.
- **Consulted.** People who provide input on a deliverable based on the impact of their work or their domain of expertise.

- **Informed.** People who need to be kept in the loop on project progress.

The RACI framework allows you to begin with the insights you've gathered, assign activities to those insights, and measure the results of those activities so that everyone is on the same page.

Not only does this system help capture and document these activities and create meaningful forward movement, it also serves as a handy reference guide. The committee chair can glance at the framework, immediately understand what actions were recommended in the previous meeting and who's responsible for what, and check in with the appropriate people.

As an example, in a recent committee meeting, one of my clients captured three very specific actions tied to the win-loss findings from the previous month. One of those actions was to train the sales team on how to explain their pricing model in a clear and concise manner since, apparently, they were struggling to do so. As a result, the committee set a thirty-day timeline to deliver the pricing training and assigned the following people to each RACI position:

- **Responsible:** Director, Sales Enablement
- **Accountable:** Director, Product Marketing
- **Consulted:** CRO
- **Informed:** Committee

The result? The training was delivered, and buyer feedback on the company's pricing model improved immediately. It was easy to measure the change in sentiment from pre-training to post-training.

COMMUNICATE IMPACT

All your hard work, and all the positive change your program generates, needs to be communicated throughout the organization. To communicate that change, I've found it's best to focus on four key areas: foundational work, strategic goals, high-impact projects, and targeted initiatives.

Next, plot these four areas into quadrants using "effectiveness and efficiency gains" as your Y-axis and "effect on revenue" as your X-axis, as illustrated in Figure 21.3.

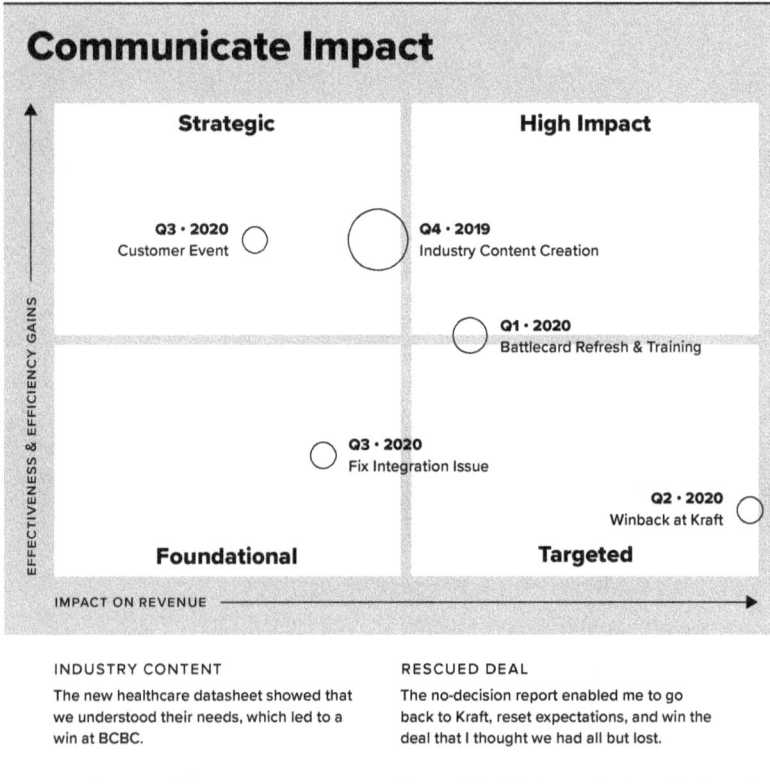

Communicate Impact

Strategic

High Impact

Q3 · 2020
Customer Event

Q4 · 2019
Industry Content Creation

Q1 · 2020
Battlecard Refresh & Training

Q3 · 2020
Fix Integration Issue

Q2 · 2020
Winback at Kraft

Foundational

Targeted

EFFECTIVENESS & EFFICIENCY GAINS

IMPACT ON REVENUE

INDUSTRY CONTENT
The new healthcare datasheet showed that we understood their needs, which led to a win at BCBC.

RESCUED DEAL
The no-decision report enabled me to go back to Kraft, reset expectations, and win the deal that I thought we had all but lost.

Figure 21.3

By plotting results along this chart, anyone can quickly and easily understand the impact that a specific initiative had. One action may have had a dramatic impact on revenue, while another may have had a significant impact on effectiveness and efficiency. The actions that achieved both? Those represent the biggest feathers in your cap—the coveted high-impact projects.

To be clear, an action doesn't need to fall into the high-impact quadrant to be valuable to your organization. Fixing an integration issue (Fig. 21.3) may not dramatically impact either revenue or effectiveness and efficiency, but it still addresses an important need—which means it ultimately moves your company forward.

THIS IS WHERE THE MAGIC HAPPENS

If it seems straightforward, even obvious, to you that you need a structured plan to act on and communicate the results of your win-loss program, congratulations! You'd be surprised how many people get close to the finish line but fail to take the steps I've outlined here.

Driving change is important, but it's also an uphill slog. It's not always easy dragooning busy people onto a new committee, but it's worth the effort.

If you've followed the book this far but you're not seeing results that reflect the quality of your interviews and insights, there are a few potential problems to consider:

- The program chair doesn't have as much influence as you'd hoped and cannot persuade committee members to act.
- You haven't sufficiently sold committee members on potential program benefits. They lack conviction, so their commitment is lacking.
- You have a naysayer in your midst. If one influential committee member doesn't believe in the program and lets others know it, the dominoes—and your support—begin to tumble.

Remember the scenarios at the beginning of this chapter? Ultimately, the success of any program depends on the human element—how well people understand and appreciate your goals and how willing they are to participate in them. Don't be the lone wolf whose research gathers dust; the more cheerleading you can do for your win-loss program—even after your committee gets underway—the greater the impact you'll have.

And how do you keep expanding your program and driving results? That just so happens to be the subject of our final chapter.

ACTIONS & TAKEAWAYS

1. After collecting all this data and conducting meaningful analysis, the last thing you want is for all the insights to die on the vine. As part of your win-loss program, it's essential you also have a plan for action.

2. I've found the best path to action is to form a win-loss committee, a group of cross-functional stakeholders who can coordinate action and hold each other accountable.

3. Generally speaking, action should be focused on things that are either easy fixes or can move the needle the most for the company. Not everything should be a big swing, but everything should lead to a clear, measurable outcome.

CHAPTER 22

Keeping Your Program Fresh and Relevant

NOT LONG AGO, I WAS WORKING WITH A CLIENT THAT WAS THE undisputed leader in its niche. The client was very comfortable as Number One—until one day when, out of the blue, Number Two (that is, its closest competitor) was bought out by yet another player in the market, Number Three.

The marriage of numbers Two and Three changed everything. Practically overnight, this newly merged company became dramatically more appealing to customers—and a much bigger threat to Number One. It's no surprise, then, that they were freaking out.

As my client, Number One had questions, and they needed quick answers. How would customers now perceive Number Two? What was the buzz? Should Number One respond aggressively, or sit back and play it cool?

I didn't know, but I knew how to find out.

Immediately, I designed an interview program to gather as much intelligence as possible for my client. Priorities had changed suddenly and unpredictably, and their win-loss program had to follow suit.

With any research program—with any *program,* really—there's a risk that things will begin to feel stale after a while. When your program is new, stakeholders are excited about all the new information they're picking up, actionable insights the organization has never been privy to before.

But time passes. People get blasé. "Yup. Been there, done that. Heard it before. Tell me something I don't know."

This attitude can kill a win-loss program. It's up to you to avoid the problem and keep things fresh, compelling, and fluid.

To do this, you'll need to be flexible and light on your feet. You'll need the agility to organically follow the information wherever it may lead. Here, in the final chapter of this book, we'll explore some possible paths to sustained vitality.

BE ADAPTIVE

Just like we did with Number One, one of the most important ways to keep your program fresh and relevant is to switch up what you're trying to learn. If you have a lot of data on the buying process, for instance, maybe it's time to focus on product feedback for a while.

In other words, think of each of the interview topics we discussed in Part 2 as part of a variable pie chart, one in which each slice grows or shrinks depending on your current needs.

These needs can change for a variety of reasons. Number One suddenly needed to understand a lot more about their newly strengthened competitor. Another client noticed early in their first round of interviews that their pricing structure was confusing prospective buyers. Curious to get more focused data, they adjusted their pie so pricing became a significant part of the conversation. Then, they defined a clear set of questions in order to get further intelligence:

- How does pricing in general affect their buying decision?
- What models work? What models don't?
- Do they prefer user-based or consumption-based pricing?

- Is there a particular competitor whose pricing structure they prefer?

All this newly focused data made its way into the company's next round of reports, allowing my client to share fresh insights with the executive team and start some much-needed conversations about pricing. Not only did this help the company solve an important problem, it provided continued validation for the win-loss program in stakeholders' eyes.

None of this would have happened if their win-loss program wasn't adaptive to changing circumstances. This is the core competency of any win-loss program owner: being able to discern important trends from the mountains of win-loss data and steer the program in the direction of those trends.

You will always have a core set of questions that remain consistent, but the only way to continue delivering value in the eyes of your stakeholders is to switch things up from quarter to quarter.

- Dive deep into any trends your interviews may unearth.
- Stay abreast of strategic objectives and competitive-intelligence efforts and fine-tune your program to deliver relevant insights.
- Collect data strategically in order to keep stakeholders informed.

Remember, as soon as you start getting that "same old, same old" vibe from your stakeholders, that's a red flag. It means you're not doing enough with the information you're collecting. You're not solving problems. Inaction at this stage will doom your win-loss program to failure. To keep it alive, keep it relevant—and keep it focused on driving action (see the previous chapter).

KNOW WHEN CHANGE IS NEEDED

Nothing stays fresh forever. How will you know when it's time to change things up?

Lean on your committee.

If you followed the advice in chapters 3 and 4, you've put in a lot of work, right from the program's earliest days, building a cross-functional committee to ensure you deliver value.

Remember, one of the committee's prime responsibilities is to determine the direction of the program. Don't be afraid to ask for guidance, and don't reflexively resist when the committee does hint at (or demand) a shift. They're doing their job, and by keeping these important stakeholders happy, you'll extend the useful life of the program.

There's a lot you can do to keep your win-loss program relevant on your own. You can learn to read trends in the win-loss data to refocus your interviews. You can keep a close eye on organizational needs and events and adjust accordingly. Consider your committee to be a valuable resource in these efforts as well. After all, they have an up-to-the-minute understanding of your organization's current priorities, and they can help deploy this knowledge to steer your win-loss program in the right direction.

PRO TIP

While a lot of your job involves *reacting* to information gleaned from your win-loss interviews, you also want to be *proactive*, anticipating major events and getting ahead of them and focusing your questions accordingly.

One good way to do this? Simply check the corporate calendar. Maybe there's a product launch in March or a new sales methodology set to take effect in September. By acting well in advance, you can design interviews that offer timely insights aligned with those events.

A PROGRAM, NOT A PROJECT

I'm sometimes asked whether a win-loss program ever runs its course—is there a time to declare victory and wrap things up?

Sure. If all of the following conditions are true, then go ahead and close up shop.

- The market stops changing.
- Your sales reps and sales process are perfect.
- Your competitors stop developing new products.
- Your customers' needs stop shifting.
- Governments stop toying with regulations.

If you're having trouble picking up on the sarcasm, I'll spell it out for you. There's never a time to wrap up your win-loss program.

The reason is right there in the name: win-loss *program*. Projects end. Programs are ongoing.

You wouldn't suggest wrapping up company efforts to improve the user experience, would you? Or to stop adding new integrations? Or to cease strengthening the channel partner ecosystem? Of course not. These are all essential programs in your company, and effective programs have no "sell by" date. Correctly gathered, analyzed, and presented, win-loss information will always deliver value to your organization.

Not long ago, during a win-loss call for a client, I was on the phone with a high-profile chief information security officer for a huge New York financial firm. The CISO was explaining why he had passed on my client's solution—because he hadn't settled on *any* solution. He casually said, "Have your client's CEO give me a call. If he can make some tweaks to his solution, he's got my business."

Had that client abandoned (or failed to develop) their win-loss program, that conversation never would have taken place. However, because they committed to their win-loss program, their efforts opened the door for a massive potential sale to a well-connected industry leader.

If you, or anybody in your company, starts to question the value of your win-loss program, it's a good indicator you need to stir things up. Maybe you haven't adapted your interview questions to the current business climate. Maybe your report deliverables need freshening up. Maybe your interviewers aren't preparing sufficiently. It's your job to address these and other variables to keep the program relevant.

Is that easy? Definitely not. Running a business is like playing a game of Whack-A-Mole. The moment you solve (at least temporarily) one problem, three others pop up.

This is true even if you have a robust, healthy win-loss program. Without a healthy win-loss program, each new problem could catch you completely by surprise. *With* a healthy win-loss program, you'll have a fighting chance not only to anticipate where those problems might pop up, but to get your hammer ready and plan your attack.

ACTIONS & TAKEAWAYS

1. Your win-loss program isn't a project. It's a program. However, this ongoing work should not remain static. Organizational priorities change, markets change, and so should your program.

2. You don't need to drive this change alone. Remember that win-loss committee you formed in the last chapter? Lean on them for direction.

Conclusion

WELL, THERE YOU HAVE IT. YOU HAVE READ THIS BOOK, IMPLE-mented a world-class win-loss program, ensured that it will be around for thousands of years, and impressed the hell out of not only your boss but your boss's boss all the way up to the C-suite. At this point, I picture you standing astride the globe, arms folded, with your super-hero cape fluttering behind you.

Hey, an author can dream, can't he?

Truly, though, we've covered a massive amount of ground in these twenty-two chapters. Chances are you grabbed this book out of something like desperation. Already busy as hell, you were asked to create a program that few people in the organization valued or even understood.

By now, you should understand not only the value a well-designed win-loss program delivers but also how to get it up and running in your company.

When I first began learning about the quantity and quality of data and insights that a win-loss program can deliver, I was shocked. Even more, I was shocked at how few businesses took advantage of these programs. We live in a business climate where data is prized above all else, and yet somehow, this particular area of inquiry has largely been overlooked.

Kind of amazing, isn't it?

Now that you've read this book, you're in on the secret. You know how to gather win-loss data, and you know how to put it to work—whether to improve the performance of your sales reps, dial in the features on the company website, or bring more focus to product design and marketing.

Of course, gathering the data is only part of the equation. If there's one thing you take away from this book, it should be this: all the data in the world won't help you if you can't package and present it in a way that's useful to your stakeholders.

Show them what you know—and more importantly, what they can do with what you know—and then sit back and watch as your company slowly conquers the world.

Finally, while this book will set you on the right path, you'll likely come across unexpected challenges. I've seen it all, so rest assured, beyond these pages there's plenty more to help you navigate choppy waters. The help doesn't stop here. As your trusty guide, I'm committed to your success. Find me on LinkedIn, reach out, tell me about your journey. I love solving problems, and I would love to hear about your successes!

Acknowledgments

TO THE MANY WHO'VE SHARED IN AND CONTRIBUTED TO MY WIN-loss journey and made this book possible—you know who you are.

To my DoubleCheck and Klue families, for your relentless belief and conviction in our cause.

To my family, who is always by my side, lifting me up, especially my kiddos Leo, Maya, and Allana.

Finally, my heartfelt thanks to Chas Hoppe, without whom this book would never have seen the light of day.

About the Author

RYAN SORLEY is the VP of Win-Loss and co-founder of Klue and a leading authority on win, loss, and churn research programs. Ryan and his team design, build, and run third-party win-loss programs for progressive B2B tech and manufacturing companies, enabling them to make smarter go-to-market decisions and stay ahead of the competition. Prior to joining Klue, Ryan spent over fifteen years at leading research firms like Gartner, AMR Research, and Forrester. In 2014, Ryan founded win-loss research firm DoubleCheck Research, which was later acquired by Klue. He hosts the *Blindspots* podcast from his home outside of Boston, where he lives with his family and not-so-mini bernedoodle, Meeko.

www.ingramcontent.com/pod-product-compliance
Lightning Source LLC
Chambersburg PA
CBHW030501210326
41597CB00013B/752